D0430454

THE LAW SCHOOL ADMISSION GAME

Play Like An Expert

Second Edition
The New, Updated, and Expanded Version of the
Amazon Bestselling Law School Admission Guide

by

ANN K. LEVINE, ESQ.

THE LAW SCHOOL
ADMISSION GAME

CONTENTS

ACKNOWLEDGMENTS 7

INTRODUCTION. 9

CHAPTER 1: THINKING ABOUT LAW SCHOOL 13

CHAPTER 2: GETTING READY TO APPLY. 17

CHAPTER 3: YOUR GPA 23

CHAPTER 4: THE LSAT 35

CHAPTER 5: APPLICATION CHECKLIST. 57

CHAPTER 6: LETTERS OF RECOMMENDATION 61

CHAPTER 7: BUILDING YOUR RESUME. 75

CHAPTER 8: EVALUATING YOUR STRENGTHS 87

CHAPTER 9: EXPLAINING YOUR WEAKNESSES 95

CHAPTER 10: THE PERSONAL STATEMENT 111

CHAPTER 11: WRITING OPTIONAL ESSAYS 135

CHAPTER 12: THE APPLICATION TIMELINE. 143

CHAPTER 13: FILLING OUT APPLICATIONS 153

CHAPTER 14: CHOOSING A LAW SCHOOL 157

CHAPTER 15: INTERVIEWS 169

CHAPTER 16: WAITLISTS, DEFERRALS, HOLDS,
    AND RESERVE LISTS 173

CHAPTER 17: TAKING TIME OFF
    BEFORE LAW SCHOOL 181

CHAPTER 18: SCHOLARSHIPS 185

CHAPTER 19: TRANSFERRING
    LAW SCHOOLS 189

CHAPTER 20: HIRING A LAW SCHOOL
    ADMISSION CONSULTANT 193

CHAPTER 21: LAW SCHOOL ADVICE 199

RESOURCES 205

APPENDIX A: SAMPLE RESUMES 207

ABOUT THE AUTHOR 221

ACKNOWLEDGMENTS

I am grateful to the following clients for giving me feedback on my first draft of this book: Zoe Friedlander, Elvira Kras, Nataly Laufer, Rebecca Sivitz (who has now helped me with all three of my books!), Stephen Pedersen, Jeff Smith, and Erin Staab.

I would also like to thank my colleagues for their contributions: Ronald Den Otter, Nathan Fox, and Matthew Riley. Feedback from Jocelyn Glantz and Elisha Alcantara was incredibly valuable. I am happy, honored, and grateful to have them on the Law School Expert, Inc. team. Thanks also to my aunt, Ruth Bloom, for her editing skills and willingness to accommodate my schedule.

Without the support I receive at home from my husband, Brent, and my daughters Haley and Nicole, and Therese Boberg, I would not have been able to fit writing this book into my schedule.

Thanks to Marni Lennon for believing in me since I was a 1L, and for continuing our friendship and adding her perspective throughout the book.

A shout out also to Lisa Jacobson, whose example and advice through the years have inspired me to continue building and dreaming.

And, three books later, I still thank Gary J. Hill for firing me, Cindy Rold for teaching me to become a perfectionist, and

Phillip Manns for trusting me to be a 26-year old Director of Admissions. Without each of them, I could not in good conscience call myself "The Law School Expert."

INTRODUCTION

SO, you're applying to law school. Like so many applicants, you could choose to wing it—do it blindly and take that leap of faith hoping you're doing it right. Or you could recognize that the decisions to go to law school and where to go to law school are ones that will follow you throughout your life. That's why putting effort into applying to law school is vital to a successful outcome. After all, the bitter lawyers (and yes, there are quite a few) are usually those who did not do their research, did not give themselves options, and did not make smart decisions.

This book is focused on helping you make great decisions about every part of the law school application process. *How do I know this?* Because I've written this book before! The first edition of *The Law School Admission Game: Play Like an Expert* has been the bestselling law school guidebook on Amazon.com ever since its publication in June 2009. Thousands of copies have sold in print, electronic, and audiobook forms. As of this printing, it has more than 80 5-star reviews (and hardly any with fewer stars), and the feedback I receive from law school applicants is gracious, appreciative, and enthusiastic. This expanded version has new and updated information to make your decisions easier and your applications more effective. A major bonus is that it is more relevant for the current economy where applications to law school are significantly declining (down 38 percent over two years as of this printing).

In addition to providing you with insider knowledge and concrete advice about putting together your law school applications (whether you are bound for Harvard or Florida Coastal or anywhere in between), there are more samples of written materials, more examples of how people have presented themselves successfully, and updates to reflect the current climate (and mechanics) for law school admissions.

As Director of Admissions for two ABA-approved law schools, I reviewed thousands of law school applications and made admission and scholarships decisions. Nearly ten years ago, I started Law School Expert, a law school admission consulting company. In that capacity, I have helped approximately 2,000 law school applicants through the admission process. The guidance in this book is shaped by and benefits from the advice, experience, and feedback from my clients who become successful law students and lawyers. Their law school experiences have run the gamut: my clients (as a whole) have been admitted to every ABA-approved law school[1] in the country.

In this book, you will learn everything you need to know to apply to law school, including:

- What the LSAT exam entails, what you should do to prepare for it, and how to select an LSAT prep program.
- How you can best use your time in college to set yourself up to be competitive for admission to law school (and to top law schools).

---

[1] Although some states have State Bar accredited law schools, I do not (as part of my law school admission consulting practice) help people with those applications.

- Issues unique to INTERNATIONAL and NON-TRADITIONAL[2] applicants.
- Who should be writing letters of recommendation on your behalf, and what they should say about you.
- A thorough explanation of the different directions you can take with your law school personal statement, and how to use this opportunity to present yourself and maximize your opportunity to impress law schools.
- How to explain potential weaknesses in your background, including those pesky "character and fitness" questions (that require you to report minor in possession tickets, DUIs, honor code violations, and sometimes even speeding tickets), disappointing grades or LSAT scores, disabilities (physical or emotional), or other obstacles overcome.
- What the *rolling admission process* really is all about, how to take advantage of it, whether it's in your best interest to apply Early Decision or Early Notification, when to take the LSAT, and when to apply to law school.
- How to deal with those intimidating secondary and optional essays including diversity statements, "Why this law school," open-ended 250 word essays, "Tell us about your favorite literary character," and other essays that schools may ask for.
- How to choose where to apply to law school based on your credentials and goals.

---

[2] Throughout the book, I will capitalize "INTERNATIONAL" and "NON-TRADITIONAL" where I am providing advice specific to applicants who fall into these categories. NON-TRADITIONAL applicants are those who have spent either more than two years out of school before applying to law school or who took a path through college that was not straight out of a high school and finishing in four years.

- The mechanics of completing applications and sending in materials to Law School Admissions Council— LSAC.org (your soon-to-be favorite website).
- How to interact with representatives of law schools during forum and recruiting events, campus visits, and interview opportunities.
- What to do if you are waitlisted.
- Choosing where to attend and how to negotiate scholarships.

That's a lot of ground to cover. So let's get started.

****

Chapter 1

THINKING ABOUT LAW SCHOOL

THERE was a time when law school was a great default option for bright college graduates who were not on the pre-med track. If you have someone paying the bill for you to attend, this could still be the case. However, in the new post-2009 economy, choosing to attend law school comes with more uncertainty and necessitates a thorough review of your strengths and weaknesses, your career aspirations, your financial situation, and your prospects given where you would be eligible to attend law school. If you have not started any serious research about the legal profession, what lawyers do, how much lawyers make, and how hard they work, you may want to begin by reading my other book, *The Law School Decision Game: A Playbook for Prospective Lawyers* (also available at Amazon.com).

If you are still in the investigation stage, this is the time to learn about law school and careers in law.

Here are some ideas for helping to further your exploration:

- Take some law-related and/or writing and research intensive courses and see how you do;
- Consider shadowing a lawyer or interning with a lawyer for a better view of the daily realities of the legal profession;
- Reach out to lawyers for informational interviews and informal meetings;
- Take a career assessment test, usually available in your school's career placement office;
- If you are a NON-TRADITIONAL applicant, talk with friends who are lawyers and people who practice law in a way that is related to your current industry or in the industry you hope to enter.

These skills are relevant and helpful in the practice of law:

- Oral and written communication skills
- Problem-solving skills
- Research skills
- People skills
- Foreign language proficiency
- Business acumen
- Willingness to work hard
- Professional ethics
- Resilience
- Being detail oriented.

The skills most utilized by lawyers can vary according to the type of practice. Litigators need to be writers and orators, but they also may need knowledge of medical records or accounting documents. Transactional attorneys need to be wordsmiths, but also may need the people skills to be deal-makers. (For more about different areas of law, see Part III of *The Law School Decision Game.*)

If you decide law school is for you, then it's time to start thinking about what the process of applying entails.

Chapter 2

GETTING READY TO APPLY

NOW that you've decided to apply to law school, it is essential to understand everything you need to take care of and how much time to give yourself to complete those tasks. If you try to go directly from deciding to apply to actually applying without understanding the importance of each part of the application process, you are setting yourself up for failure.

The two most important factors in law school admission are your undergraduate GPA and your LSAT score. There are *no* exceptions to this; I would be lying if I told you otherwise. *Why?* Statistically, these are the best predictors of your ability to succeed in law school. Each law school keeps statistics on their students, how they perform in law school, and the extent to which their entrance credentials were in line with their performance. Law schools can actually use these statistics to determine your likelihood of success in law school and your likelihood to pass the bar on the first try. Generally, law schools want to make solid bets: will you be able to compete in the classroom given who else will be there? You need something (LSAT or GPA usually) to make the case that you can, in fact, compete.

Many law schools make exceptions on the numbers. In

fact, I could even go so far as to say that all law schools make exceptions on the numbers, and I would still be right. However, law schools feed the student data to LSAC, which in turn produces correlation studies to show who makes it through law school and who passes the bar on the first try. The data are used by *U.S.News and World Reports* to rank law schools, so law schools are extremely numbers-conscious. You need to have an outstanding application to become an exception. How do you know whether you might fall into this category? Read on.

As you go through this process, it is critical to cultivate resources you can trust. There is so much information out there in the Internet universe, and you need to evaluate who is giving the advice. *Also, it's important to remember that not all situations are universal:* the right advice for someone who is probably going to Harvard Law is not necessarily the right advice for someone hoping to go to their neighborhood law school, part-time, while supporting a family. Throughout this book, I address the issues law school applicants face with their various goals and diverse backgrounds.

If you are thinking about applying to law school, the basics are as follows:

- You must have a bachelor's degree before you start law school.
- You must take the LSAT and have a score within three years (for most schools, although a few will accept a score received within the past five years).
- The law school you attend matters. A lot. It dictates your career opportunities and earning potential. For more on this, you should read *The Law School Decision Game.*

If you are still in college, here is some advice for setting yourself up to be successful in the law school application process:

- *Work hard, pick classes that interest and excite you, and do well in the most challenging classes you can.* It usually helps to study something in which you have a sincere interest. "This is one of the best ways of acquiring the knowledge and developing the skills that will enable you to excel as a law student," according to Ronald Den Otter, pre-law advisor at Cal Poly San Luis Obispo and a graduate of the University of Pennsylvania Law School.

- *Build relationships with your professors.* Take the initiative to visit them during office hours, to take more than one class with a professor, and/or to assist in a professor's research to cultivate great letters of recommendation when you need them (and in order to benefit fully from your undergraduate experience).

- *Don't join anything just because you think it looks good.* If something really interests you, become an active leader in the organization. It doesn't have to be the pre-law club. Whether it's a cultural organization, student government, a volunteer organization, or athletics, think about how you demonstrate leadership, growth, and dedication in your involvements rather than simply collecting memberships in a number of different groups.

- *Find your niche.* Use the opportunities presented to you in college to explore things that really interest you, no matter how prestigious they seem to others. Test your boundaries and stretch your horizons, whether you run races, photograph India's villages, or participate in Alternative Spring Break programs.

- *Continue working on your grades during your senior year, just in case you don't end up going to law school right out of college.* Law schools will see these grades.
- *Conduct yourself professionally.* This includes how you present yourself on social networking sites. Use appropriate e-mail addresses and enforce privacy settings. ("Admission officers have told me that they have looked at certain applicants' Facebook pages," said one pre-law advisor.) Most of my clients change their Facebook names while they are applying to law school and while this confuses me greatly when I read my newsfeed every day, I think it's a smart idea. Law schools are looking for indicators of professionalism. One law school administrator told me that she pulled a scholarship from a prospective student based on Facebook content. "Before offers are made, I search online. It's a reality," she said.
- *Stay out of trouble.* Be careful about your conduct in the dorms and around campus. There's no reason to fight with your R.A. and get a discipline record over a noise violation in the dorm. Show that you exercise good judgment by not finding yourself in situations where you are getting citations for underage drinking, use of fake IDs, etc. If this advice is coming too late, make up for it by taking responsibility for your actions and not becoming a repeat offender. (See Chapter 9, "Explaining Your Weaknesses.")
- *Consider things and don't just follow a prescribed pattern.* Be honest with yourself: choosing activities

isn't about what your mom can brag about. It's about deciding what you like, what you're good at, and what you'd like to know more about. When you observe your experiences candidly, what do you see? Are you someone who never really had to earn her own pocket money? You might benefit from real, roll-up-your-sleeves work experience. Do you appear to be a little self-centered by being active only in your fraternity? How can you use that involvement to reach out to others? Do you need to compensate for lackluster grades by demonstrating intellectual ability? Perhaps you should pursue a research project, a thesis, or even tutoring other students in a subject where you are strong. If you have always had "the right" internships with politicians, consider getting down and dirty with the people addressing problems on the ground level. Taking time for introspection now will not only benefit your law school applications, but will encourage your personal growth. This will, in turn, help you make good decisions about your future.

- *Spend your summers wisely.* Explore different careers. Explore the world. Not everything on your resume needs to have a direct connection with law: business skills are important, too! Learning how to function in a professional environment, learning how to live on your own far from home, learning a language, and even saving money for a certain goal (backpacking in Europe or saving for your next semester's tuition) are worthy activities for a summer during college. If you decide to work in a law firm, make sure you do more than file and answer phones: take time to actually talk to lawyers about what they do on a daily basis. Turn everything into a real learning experience, and you will grow and expand your horizons. Whatever you do, don't phone it in. Engage with it!

For those of you who are NOT still in college, here are some tips for NON-TRADITIONAL applicants as they get ready to apply to law school:

- *Look creatively for writers of recommendations:* If you are working but not comfortable letting your employer know that you are thinking of leaving, then you will need to think creatively about who should write letters of recommendation; you may need to add a volunteer position and/or a class to try to cultivate an appropriate letter of recommendation.
- *Save money:* LSAT preparation and applications (and admission consulting) may eat up your discretionary funds if you're not prepared for the expense.
- *Research your career expectations:* older applicants face a different set of issues when deciding whether a law career is feasible given their family demands and the age at which they might hope to retire.

Chapter 3

YOUR GPA

L AW school is academically rigorous, no matter where you go. So, it's important to demonstrate that you can handle yourself in the classroom. This is why grades are so important. Grades *should* be the best indicator of how you will perform in law school (although this certainly isn't true for everyone, and law schools do appreciate that). You must send all of your transcripts (with exceptions for study abroad and other unique circumstances as noted on the LSAC.org website) to LSAC. They will be evaluated according to certain guidelines that try to prevent graduates of any one college's grading system to be at an advantage over graduates from any other college. Your grades are then calculated and your new LSAC cumulative (and degree) GPA will be sent (along with your transcripts) with each law school application you submit.

If there were circumstances that interfered with your ability to perform to your potential in college, including trauma, serious illness, underlying disability, or otherwise, there are ways to address this in the application. (See Chapter 9, Explaining Weaknesses.) However, you cannot ignore the impact of your GPA even with these factors. It is important to understand how law schools will interpret your degree and your academic performance.

What Transcripts Do I Need to Send to LSAC?

All of your transcripts, post-high school level, need to go to LSAC, except any study abroad programs of short duration.[3] You need to follow the instructions at LSAC.org *exactly* to avoid delays in having your applications processed. Denial won't help you: you can't avoid sending the summer school transcripts from junior college even if you took the credits while still in high school. That class you forgot to withdraw from will count, too! If you are currently in school, you can send updated transcripts at the end of the next term. NON-TRADITIONAL applicants should go ahead and send transcripts as soon as possible to find out their LSAC-calculated GPA. If you are still in college, and applying in the fall, go ahead and send the transcripts you have through your junior year/summer before senior year. Does that mean you can fool around during your senior year? NO! Law schools will want updated transcripts as the application season progresses and will need to see your final transcripts before you enroll. If you are concerned that you haven't had time to pull your grades up, consider taking a year off after college and then applying to law school. Law schools will then have to consider grades from your entire senior year.

It can take three weeks for transcripts to be processed at LSAC, and that's only after your undergraduate school (or schools!) finally send your transcripts. Don't wait until the week applications are due to take care of this. Your application will not be deemed complete by schools until they have all

---

[3] see www.lsac.org/jd/apply/cas-requesting-transcripts.asp for more details

transcripts. *Note:* your application will not be reviewed until it is deemed "complete."

Why Is My LSAC GPA Different from My College GPA?

Although your graduating institution may not count grades from a transferring institution in your GPA, they will be included for LSAC. As a result, there is no advantage to transferring, and a person cannot erase part of their college performance and "start over," enabling a comparison with someone who stayed at the same college for all four years. Grades with pluses or minuses may be calculated differently by LSAC than by your college. Also, repeated courses and pass/fail courses are counted differently than your undergraduate institution may count them so that no one can be at an advantage by getting another bite at the apple. Once you receive your first bachelor's degree, no more credits count toward your undergraduate GPA. Your cumulative LSAC GPA is the one schools use as your official GPA. Law schools will see your academic breakdown by year and institution through your Academic Summary Report and your transcripts.

What Does the School Do with My GPA?

Most schools take your GPA (your LSAC Cumulative GPA) and highest LSAT score (see Chapter 4, "The LSAT") and assign an index number to your file according to a formula they use to determine who is likely to succeed at their law school. This formula is based on how previous students have fared in law school and on the bar exam. Some schools simply use 25th and 75th percentile numbers as a starting point for initial file categorization. The categorization is based on that school's previous students' academic performance and their first attempt to pass the bar exam. (For more information, see http://lawschoolexpert. com/uncategorized/the-time-is-now-to-get-into-law-school-infographic/.)

Schools also consider your GPA subjectively based on a number of factors:

- Quality of undergraduate school
- Difficulty of major
- Upward trend
- Grades—Are your grades recent or do they reflect a younger version of yourself
- Explanations— any explanations you provide about a period of less impressive grades (see Chapter 9, "Explaining Your Weaknesses")

How Will Law Schools View My Major?

Law schools want to see that, when challenged academically, you rise to the occasion. There are two aspects to this: the academic challenge and rising to the occasion. Therefore, having an easier major and higher grades is not the perfect solution. There is no one perfect major that all law schools want to see; in fact, they want to enroll people from different academic backgrounds. But it's important to show your education helped you develop critical thinking skills, writing and research skills, and intellectual curiosity. Whether you studied music or chemistry or business, the most important thing to demonstrate is that you do well at the things you undertake. Below is a summary of different types of undergraduate majors and how they are viewed by law schools. I share this not to make you paranoid about your choices, but to show you what concerns law schools may have so you can think about perceived weaknesses that you can "overcome" in your personal statement and/or addendum.

Political Science, History, Philosophy, Criminal Justice, and Other Pre-Law Majors

If you majored in political science, history, philosophy, or a related field, you should have two advantages: (1) a clear demonstration of your long-standing interest in law, and (2) a good GPA. If you wrote a thesis, even better. This shows that you performed meaningful writing and research and approached your studies in a focused and serious way. However, if you don't have a strong GPA and a compelling reason for the mediocre performance (see Chapter 9, "Explaining Your Weaknesses"), then you will need to show seriousness of purpose and focus in another way (student leadership, internships, etc.). Philosophy is the more intellectual cousin of the pre-law majors, and if you do well with philosophy (and with actually making an argument with a conclusion, rather than simply making assertions or raising more questions), then it shows an academic affinity for law school, particularly at the higher end (Ivy league) universities and high LSAT levels—the Top 10 law schools definitely see this as preparation for an academic career path (becoming a law professor, etc.).

On the other side of the coin is the criminal justice major, which is seen as the trade school end of the pre-law major spectrum, especially since prestigious universities do not offer it as a major and it's seen more for people who aspire to become law enforcement and probation officers. "A 3.25 GPA in criminal justice might be equated with a 3.0 in political science or a 2.75 in the sciences," according to Charles Roboski, Assistant Dean of Admission and Financial Aid at Michigan State University

College of Law. As a consultant, I see a lot of people from John Jay College with this background and it's very hard for students to compete because of the type of education (and the hard time these students often have with the LSAT). However, because most students with a Criminal Justice major are trying to get into their regional law school rather than Harvard, it's less of an issue.

Science/Math/Engineering

Your GPA may be lower (in the 3.0 range) and still be impressive because of difficult courses and extended laboratory hours. This background will be especially helpful if you want to go into patent or intellectual property law. If you are worried about how your physics GPA will match up against the political science majors, relax. If your grades are solid, you have strong academic letters of recommendation, you attended a reputable university, and you have some evidence of writing ability, you will find yourself at no inherent disadvantage in the admission process. In fact, you may even stand out more. Schools know that grading is objective rather than subjective in these areas of study; you either know your material or you don't, so these areas are less subject to grade inflation.

Foreign Languages/Identity Studies

Good news: knowing another language (e.g., Russian, Chinese, Spanish) shows diversity. Bad news: it doesn't make you a shoo-in for "International Lawyer of the Year." If you can demonstrate the challenges of your area of study given your background, show intellectual curiosity, and demonstrate that knowledge of this particular language will allow you to serve an underrepresented group as an attorney, then you'll be in good shape. Majoring in identity studies (e.g., women's studies,

African American studies) shows intellectual curiosity but also tends to make you sound very idealistic (which works well for those of you expressing an inclination for public interest law).

Communication/Journalism

As someone who holds a Bachelor of Science in Communications, I have to say, this is seen as a soft degree: it's not particularly challenging or interesting or intellectual. So, hopefully, you can demonstrate that you honed your writing and public speaking skills highlighting examples of published work and/or investigative projects.

Education

The big question is: Why aren't you becoming a teacher? You are trained to be a teacher, and our country needs bright, capable, motivated teachers (arguably much more than we need more lawyers). So why are you applying to law school? It's important to articulate why you want to leave a valuable and respected profession you were trained and certified to enter. Trust me, I've heard the "I can do more as an advocate for education policy" and "I want to represent families trying to obtain accommodations for their children in the public school setting." This is very popular with Teach for America people as well (see Chapter 10, "The Personal Statement").

Bachelor of Fine Arts

This is tricky, since so much of your training (e.g., *theatre, dance, music, film*) was professional based rather than academic, and very difficult for professors to explain in terms of academic skills in a letter of recommendation. A letter of recommendation can go a long way toward adding credibility to your academic program. It might include how hard you had to work at your discipline and how intense the program is, your personal dedication to self-improvement, as well as your ability to work with others and to take criticism. Hard work and dedication are inherent in these majors. But the other side of the coin is the question of why you are applying to law school—it just seems so obvious and cliché that you got tired of being an out-of-work actor or musician. If you had a double major in an academic subject, you can overcome this presumption a bit, and if you did any academic writing or research, find a way to emphasize it. If you majored in art history or music composition, these show you are a thinking person, and analytical—that you can look at something or hear something and make judgments about its origin based on certain clues. Certainly, these are skills that translate well to law.

Business/Accounting

Business and law are—and should be—intertwined. After all, lawyers in private practice are all in business (like it or not) and the ability to manage a practice is a skill that is often ignored in law school but essential in law practice. Plus, lawyers advise businesses. So, there's no inherent weakness in applying to law school with a major in business. During my years practicing law, I looked at more Profit and Loss statements than Supreme Court opinions, so an understanding of accounting will be pretty darn useful (especially if you plan to manage a law firm one day).

An Economics major brings some clout because of the difficulty and intellectual nature of the courses. (Nathan Fox, lawyer and author of *Cheating the LSAT*, claims it will even help you on the LSAT.) A business management major at a selective business school is something law schools respect, especially because of the real-world aspect of the education and the team-work that is often required.

Psychology/Sociology

These fields are research-based and people-based, and you've probably done some writing, so they are fine majors for applying to law school.

How Can I Overcome Perceived Weaknesses in My Major?

Once you know how law schools view your major, think about what you can do to make up for any inherent weaknesses. If you haven't had much writing in your curriculum, try writing for the school paper, for a blog, or becoming a research assistant to a professor. For NON-TRADITIONAL applicants, this can be harder, of course, but there are still blogs to write for and other ways to show you have experience writing.

How Will Law Schools View the School(s) I Attended?

The caliber of school you attended is important. Harvard will not view a 4.0 from Kaplan University the same way it will view a 4.0 from Dartmouth, no matter how you argue it. At most law schools, a GPA above 3.2 is considered fairly respectable, especially if there is an upward trend. But a 3.7+ and mid-160s LSAT score has been getting my clients into Top 14 and Top 10 law schools recently, including Yale, University of Virginia, Harvard, Georgetown, Berkeley, University of Pennsylvania, and Cornell. However, these are people with strong academic backgrounds at prestigious undergraduate schools (including UCLA, Dartmouth, Villanova, Stanford, and University of California-Santa Barbara).

What If I Started at Community College and Transferred to a Four-Year University?

If your grades stayed strong after transferring, you are not at a great disadvantage in the admission process for most schools. A city college might not be what Columbia Law is looking for; they are comparing your grades throughout four years with people who attended Dartmouth for all four years, but starting at a community college and transferring and excelling (especially when diversity-related issues were among your reasons for attending community college in the first place) will actually be respected by law schools. If you transferred many times over several years and your grades were inconsistent, it will be important to show an upward trend.

What If I Attended College Online?

If you attended college while in the military, online courses are understandable. But if you attended Kaplan University or another for-profit institution, law schools don't put a lot of stock in your performance. However, I have seen some people write very effective explanations for why they had to attend school online and why it was actually quite rigorous because of the accountability it requires.

Should I Take More Classes to Boost My UGPA?

Courses won't count toward your GPA after you've graduated from college (for the first time, for those of you with more than one bachelor's degree). However, if it has been a long time since you attended college and you are trying to show you are a more serious student now, it can help you to take a class or two at a local college. If you do well, this can always help you to obtain an academic letter of recommendation.

Why Don't My Post-Bachelor's and Graduate Degree Grades Count?

Law schools need everyone to start on an even playing field. It wouldn't be fair to people who graduated in three years if you could keep going to college for five years to boost your GPA. Likewise, not everyone has a graduate degree, so your graduate school grades can't be used as an objective factor in your application.

What If I Have an Upward Trend in My Grades?

Law schools look favorably on people who consistently improve, understanding that some are late bloomers as they come to college. However, at Top 10 law schools you need to be consistently strong all around. Impressive grades throughout your education are essential, and a lackluster undergraduate GPA can probably be overlooked at this level only if there is significant graduate level academic work or a very credible reason for a period of poor academic performance (an injury or illness that was resolved, etc.)—or, of course, a strong LSAT score!

What If My Grades Are Consistently Mediocre?

Some excellence (in subjects related to law or other thoughtful fields) is preferred over consistent mediocrity. Your "C"s in Calculus and Organic Chemistry and even Modern Dance will be easily forgiven, but the same grades in History, Political Science, and Religion 101 will not be viewed so charitably.

Will My Study Abroad Grades Count?

For those of you who partied during study abroad, get ready to kiss me: those grades don't count toward your LSAC GPA. (I've noticed that my clients who are my Facebook friends are truly making the most of this handy fact.) For those of you who worked hard to try to bring up your GPA during a semester abroad, sorry! It's not my fault!

What If My GPA Is from a Foreign Institution? (Or, from University of California-Santa Cruz before they instituted grades?)

If you have studied only in a language other than English, you will probably need to take the TOEFL and work on the writing sample portion of the LSAT because law schools will be reading it carefully to check your fluency under pressure. Many universities in Asia rank students, and this is helpful and persuasive to law schools. Law schools also understand that there is no grade inflation in many other countries, and this can work in your favor. If you attended a college in the United States that provides evaluations rather than grades, your GPA will be calculated as a 0.00. However, schools will review your evaluations to determine whether you were a serious and committed student. In both cases (the foreign student and the evaluated student), schools will be forced to rely more heavily on your LSAT score to determine your potential to succeed.

Chapter 4

THE LSAT

YOU need to take the LSAT exam to apply to law school. There are two ways around this but they are very narrow exceptions: Northwestern's accelerated JD program that allows a GMAT instead, or a few undergraduate programs that allow you to combine a Bachelor's and JD in a 6-year program. For the other 99.9 percent, the LSAT is in your future.

The LSAT is offered four times each year (February, June, October,[4] and December). You need to register in advance. [5]

There are three major questions that you need answered and all are addressed at length in this chapter:

1. What is the LSAT?
2. When should you take it?
3. How will you prepare for it?

The LSAT is an aptitude test. It is not based on the memorization of facts, but it requires preparation to learn the question types and to develop the skills being tested.

---

[4] The fall LSAT date is sometimes at the end of September and sometimes at the beginning of October. I refer to them interchangeably throughout this book as either the September LSAT or October LSAT.

[5] To register for the LSAT online go to www.lsac.org/jd/lsat/lsat-registration-methods.asp

To assist me in this chapter (since mastery of the LSAT is beyond my expertise regarding how to get into law school), I've called on five LSAT experts:

1. Nathan Fox is a graduate of University of California-Hastings Law School and the author of *Cheating the LSAT*. He is an LSAT teacher in San Francisco. His website is www.foxtestprep.com.

2. Noah Teitelbaum is the executive director of academics at Manhattan Prep, and is featured in the online tutoring and preparation programs available through www.ManhattanLSAT.com.

3. Ben Olson is the founder of Strategy Prep (www.strategyprep.com), an LSAT preparation company in Washington, DC. Before starting Strategy, Ben earned his JD from George Washington University.

4. Jodi Teti is the president of Blueprint Test Preparation (www.blueprintprep.com).

5. John Rood is the president of Next Step Test Prep (www.nextsteptestprep.com).

For ease of reference, I'll refer to them each by first name throughout this chapter.

What Is the LSAT and What Does It Test?

There are five sections on the LSAT, but only three types of sections because one will be experimental and not graded, and one section is given twice. There is no math on the LSAT. According to Nathan, "Lawyers are gladiators who do battle with words. As such, the Law School Admission Test (LSAT) primarily tests your command of the English language. Reading and vocabulary are at a premium, just like they will be in law school and throughout your legal career. The test is comprised of three different types of sections:

1. Logical Reasoning sections ask you to support, attack, or analyze short arguments.
2. Reading Comprehension sections ask you to read long, dense passages and then answer questions about what you've read.
3. Analytical Reasoning sections, also known as "Logic Games," ask you to solve puzzles."

How Much Time Should I Set Aside for Studying?

You should spend at least two months, and perhaps as much as four, with the LSAT as a major priority in your life. "Since most students start off at different ability levels, it's somewhat difficult to generalize how long one should study for the LSAT. Our experience shows that the majority of students preparing for the LSAT should plan on 2.5 to 3.5 months of intensive LSAT preparation. What does 'intensive' mean? Students who are on this timeline should aim to carve out at least 15 hours per week to spend on LSAT prep," says Noah.

"If you are working full-time, are a full-time student, or just don't have between two and four hours per day to put toward LSAT study, then four to six months may be a better timeline," says Jodi.

"Part of what the LSAT tests is your ability to put your nose to the grindstone. You'll certainly have to do this as a law student, and even more in legal practice, so you may as well start now. One way LSAC tests your ability to work hard is by making their old tests available. There are no secrets on the LSAT! The questions change from test to test, but only super-ficially—the same concepts are tested over and over. Every student is different, but I recommend that students complete five full-length practice tests at an absolute minimum. Many students do 50 practice tests or more!" advises Nathan.

How Should I Prepare?

According to Jodi:

"Preparation includes three parts:

1. learning the techniques to tackle particular questions,
2. practicing those techniques until they become automatic,
3. applying the techniques during timed tests."

Noah suggests taking a timed practice test to get started. "This will give you a feel for the test and will provide a benchmark score from which to improve. A smart second step is to *table* the practice tests for a while, perhaps 3 to 4 weeks, in order to focus on learning and practicing sound strategies."

Jodi states that "Students who choose to study on their own might experience difficulty with learning the appropriate techniques to tackle questions because they have to formulate those techniques on their own. Prep courses can help streamline this process."

"If you're able to invest the time and money, taking a prep course or hiring a private tutor—while not essential to LSAT success—can be a smart way to go about preparing for the LSAT. A strong LSAT teacher can quickly identify where your approach is weak, push you out of your ruts, and show you how to make your study sessions more effective." Says Noah. He adds that, "Different types of students will have different preparation needs. We certainly believe in our 12-session in-person and live online courses. However, taking a course may not be feasible for everyone due to budget or schedule. At Manhattan

LSAT, we are big believers in self-study—as long as the self-studier uses a structured approach."

If I'm Going to Study on My Own, Where Do I Start?

Ben suggests starting with Nathan's book on Test 61, then working through the Powerscore Bibles. "Then take official, full-length tests, probably starting around Test 52, working your way up to the most recent LSAT (as of this printing, there have been 70). As you discover your strengths and weaknesses, use sites like cambridgelsat.com to drill specific question types. Also, find a study buddy," he says.

Nathan agrees about the value of having a study partner. "It doesn't matter if your partner has way more or way less experience than you. Both partners can still benefit. One partner learns, while the other partner learns by teaching. I actually believe that the partner doing the teaching benefits more in this arrangement; the best way to deepen understanding of a concept is to explain it to someone else. My partner and I each did practice tests on our own, then got together periodically over coffee to review our mistakes. It's simple and effective."

Noah says, "One common misconception that people have about self-studying is that they should cram in as many prep tests as possible; this is not the most efficient use of time and energy. Learning a lot of strategy first will make the prep tests that you take far more beneficial; instead of reinforcing bad habits, you will be practicing ones that will take you to your best possible score. Reviewing your prep tests in a meaningful way is as important as actually taking them; everyone knows that there's something to be learned from each wrong answer, but you can further hone your skills by reviewing correct questions that slowed you down or on which you were unable to quickly and confidently eliminate four answers. It may be wise to invest in a self-study package with a detailed syllabus and course recordings and books and prep tests."

Jodi believes that "Too often, students take timed test after timed test without seeing a score increase. This is typically because they take practice tests without first putting in the time to learn the appropriate techniques and reinforcing them through homework."

One of my former clients who is currently attending New York University Law School and scored in the low 170s on his LSAT has the following to add: "I think anyone who is serious about law school should do the full gamut: PowerScore Bibles + PowerScoreWorkbooks + Manhattan. It's an arms race, and I suspect Powerscore+Manhattan is the only way to get a really stellar (175+) score anymore (studying on your own). Another former client who is about to start law school at (coincidentally) the same law school took the Testmasters course. She told me, "It probably had a lot to do with the teacher, and outside of the course, it's really about personal discipline. You have to sit yourself down, time yourself, and review your wrong answers to make sure you're not making the same mistakes repeatedly."

Remember, however, that the LSAT is an aptitude test. I think I'm a fairly bright and capable person, and I graduated in the top ten percent of my law school class, but even if I studied for a year, I wouldn't get a 175 on the LSAT. I probably wouldn't get a 165, either. This isn't an intelligence test although intelligence will take you far on it. It's also not a test where any amount of preparation will guarantee a 99th percentile score. You'll need to work hard, no doubt. But the best you can do is become very familiar with the types of questions, perfect your timing, and reach a level of scoring that demonstrates your aptitude. This is why I tell people not to have a "goal" score before they start studying. Also, LSAT performance usually correlates to SAT performance so unless you got a near perfect score on the SAT, you are unlikely to obtain near-perfection on the LSAT.

What Should I Look for in an LSAT Prep Course?

"*Two things: Good materials and a great instructor.* The materials part is easy; as long as you're using real LSAT questions, you're off to a good start. Finding a great instructor is harder. Most LSAT teachers do the job only temporarily, picking up some quick cash while waiting for their own legal careers to begin. If you can, try to find a teacher who has fallen in love with teaching the LSAT and decided to make a career of it. Start with Yelp.com to see if there's a highly-rated LSAT provider in your area. At a minimum, you should see if you can speak to your actual instructor before plunking down $1,000 or more on a class. The big test prep companies have a mix of good, fair, and poor instructors, with a wide variety of training and experience. Ask how many classes your teacher has previously taught, and ask if you can speak to a former student of that instructor. Ask what your instructor scored on the actual LSAT, but remember that the abilities to do and to teach are two very different things. Ask whether or not the instructor graduated from law school, and if not, why not," advises Nathan.

John (whose company offers only tutoring but not prep courses) says, "The different prep courses are way more similar than they are different. Ninety-five percent of the materials are the same. There's also an arms race for how long the course is—let me tell you that you don't particularly need to be in class for 100 hours.[6] What you should look for is a great instructor. Insist on getting the specific credentials of the instructor and get references of past students. The larger the company you are considering, the less forthcoming they will be with these data."

Don't enroll in a course unless you will attend. "Commit to attending and doing the work. Courses and tutors can be invaluable, but don't fool yourself that you'll simply get a great score by signing up, or even sitting in the seat. You have to work hard to get your best score," says Noah.

What Are Things to Be Wary of in an LSAT Prep Course?

Noah offers the following advice: "Be wary of companies that create their own faux LSAT questions to save a few bucks on LSAC license fees. You're investing a lot of time and money in the class, and there's no point wasting your time on questions that never actually appeared on the test! Also, be wary of money-back guarantees. Frequently, these "guarantees" come with all sorts of restrictions that make it impossible for most students to get a refund. For example, some programs require that you attend every single class session, or do 100% of the homework, in order to be eligible for a refund."

"Do not take any course that lasts less than a month. This includes ALL courses that run only on a weekend or two weekends. These courses are essentially a cash grab aimed at students who haven't planned ahead. Second, avoid any course that doesn't assign a lot of full timed tests (proctored or not)," says John. Based on my experience, I agree: If you're not a strong

---

[6] Jodi adds the warning, "Be careful: some companies include online homework as part of the classroom hours."

standardized test taker, these courses are just enough to confuse you and to make you feel like you haven't prepared enough.

"Many LSAT classes will pile 30 or more students into an auditorium. The best way to sharpen the skills necessary to do well on the LSAT is to participate in a highly interactive, mentally intense environment. Lecture-style 'classes' are basically videos that you can't pause and rewind!" says Noah.

Ben issues a warning: "Don't think that it will be easy. The success stories you read online are probably true, but the students who wrote those stories probably worked really hard. The key to making the most of any course is to plan on doing a ton of homework outside of class—sometimes three to four hours every day you don't have class. Granted, you might not need to put in that much time every week, but some weeks you might. If you're ready to do that, you're ready to get the most out of what the course has to offer.

A client of mine who earned a score in the low 170s adds that "Simply attending class is not enough if you don't do the homework assigned."

Side note: On the flip side of this, some students put their entire social lives on hold until the test and, not surprisingly, burn out. This burnout ultimately hurts their score, so plan a fun break once a week.

How Do I Pick an LSAT Tutor?

Nathan offers the following advice:

"Start by reading reviews and talking to former students. Then talk to the tutor on the telephone or schedule a one-hour preliminary tutoring session to see what kind of rapport you have. Many people can master the LSAT, but far fewer can help someone else master it. Ask yourself: Is this person going to motivate me to study harder? Am I going to look forward to our tutoring sessions? Would I feel comfortable calling this person for extra help when I'm feeling frustrated? Does this person genuinely care about my progress, or are they just doing a job? Remember that you often get what you pay for when hiring a professional. Hourly rates don't correlate perfectly with teaching ability, but the fact that a tutor is able to command a certain rate in the marketplace usually does indicate skill, experience, and a satisfied client base. If a tutor who charges twice as much gives you three times the improvement, then that's a good value. Finally, ask how much of your tutoring fee goes directly to the tutor. Big prep companies usually take a huge chunk of a tutor's fee off the top. So a tutor who you're paying $150 per hour might only get $50 of that. Are you getting full value from this arrangement? Or would you be better off paying the entire $150 to an independent tutor, who might be more highly skilled and more deeply invested in your success?"

Yes, the tutor/instructor should have done well on the LSAT, but more importantly he or she needs to have experience teaching others to do well on the LSAT. A background in teaching people from different backgrounds is very important, especially for test takers with learning disabilities. "The very worst LSAT instructor is the 178-scorer who just has no idea why a 145 student doesn't understand the material," according to John.

"Ask to meet him or her in person; most tutors will offer to meet for free. When you meet, ask him or her to show you how to approach a hard logic game or a hard logical reasoning question so you can see if you like his or her teaching style," advises Ben.

How Much Can I Expect to Improve from an Initial Diagnostic Score?

I get phone calls all the time from people who are panicking after taking their first practice test and score in the low 140s. Ben notes that "How much you improve depends largely on how much effort you put into practicing. But assuming you work hard, almost everyone can go up 5 points. About half can go up 8 to 12 points. And some can go up 15 points or more. How much you improve also depends on where you start. Going from 152 to 162, for example, is usually easier than going from 162 to 172. In general, the hill gets steeper as you go up."

It can be harder to improve on Reading Comprehension (since that's not a new skill) than on Logic Games, according to Nathan. "The scale is also hard to climb in the middle. It will take two more questions correct to move up by a single LSAT point. Closer to the top of the scale, one more question correct generally equals one more LSAT point. The Easiest student to help improve is the one who walks in with a 162 starting score but has no clue on the Logic Games. This student will almost always end up in the 170s, given enough time," says Nathan.

Do I really have the potential to score in the 170+ range? According to Ben, "When someone who has never seen an LSAT before scores 160 or higher on a first practice test, that person has a very good chance of hitting 170. That said, I've seen many students who have scored lower than that on their first LSAT and end up breaking 170. I've seen a few students who started in the 140s reach 170. That's rare, so don't plan on it. But a big part of their success was persistence. Even though they didn't reach their goal in the typical two or three months many students take to prepare, they worked their way up to the mid-150s, and then worked their way to the mid-160s, and then worked their way up over 170."

Now that you've heard from some LSAT test experts, let me give you my expert opinion on LSAT test *strategy* (when, where, why, and whether to take the test).

Tips on How the LSAT Fits into Your Application Strategy

Choose an LSAT Date—This Is an Important First Step.

If you are a junior in college planning to attend law school immediately after college graduation, then you should plan to take the LSAT either in June after your junior year (assuming you have time to study for it during the spring semester/quarter) or in October of your senior year (giving you the chance to study for it during the summer). If you are a senior in college planning to take a year off before law school, the October LSAT also gives you the summer to prepare. This plan means that if something doesn't go as intended, you can still take the December LSAT as a backup and apply in good time. (See Chapter 12, "The Application Timeline.") Remember, it takes 3 to 4 weeks after the test to receive your score so you need to plan for that delay.

For NON-TRADITIONAL applicants, you need to judge your work and family responsibilities to decide the best time to take the test. You may want to consider using some vacation time a day or two a week for the six weeks before the test and/or taking a few days off before the test to relax and focus.

Do NOT Take This Test BLIND OR COLD.

See how I put NOT, BLIND, and OR COLD in ALL CAPS? I'm not freaking kidding.[7] Planning to take the test just to see what happens? *Big Mistake. Huge.* (Most of you are too young to understand the *Pretty Woman* reference here but indulge me anyway.) The LSAT is hugely important. (It's not everything, it's true. For example, just today, one of my clients with a 150 LSAT got into both George Washington and Hastings.) But, never doubt that it counts for a hell of a lot. Don't mess around: it is three or six months of preparation that has a huge part of determining your future career opportunities and how much you will pay for your law degree.[8]

Plan to Take the LSAT Once and Do It Right.

That's the right attitude. I often quote *Sweet Home Alabama*, "You can't ride two horses with one ass, sugarbean." Make one plan and commit to it. If it doesn't work out because life gets in the way or your have a bad test day, it's perfectly acceptable to take the LSAT a second and even a third time.

Sign Up Early.

If you don't sign up early, you may not get a testing location that is convenient for you.

---

[7] A former client who gave me feedback on an early draft of this book specifically requested that I include "an extra super-sized dose of Ann Levine Brutal Honesty™" (His words, not mine). I hope this fulfills his request sufficiently.

[8] You might also surprise yourself and really grow to like the challenges presented in the test. One of my clients who scored in the 170s told me, "It really challenges the way that you think, and it's honestly fun to figure out a tough logic game."

Don't Study On Your Own—Especially If You Struggle with Standardized Tests.

In addition, I find that people who underperform on standardized tests (under 50th percentile) do not do well in big LSAT prep courses. The money is better put toward tutoring for these individuals, but then again only if the tutor is an experienced educator. Someone who naturally does well on standardized tests should not be hired to teach the LSAT based solely on a test score—that is definitely not an indicator of ability to explain things to people who struggle with these concepts.

Remember: Hardly Any Schools Average LSAT Scores.

If the schools say they do, they are—sort of—lying.

Study amid Chaos.

One of my favorite former clients (who signed up to work with me after reading the first version of this book and who actually did so without ever even calling me first— crazy guy!) says, "I took tests cold, hot, indoors, outdoors, in Starbucks, in sports bars from 10 p.m. to 2 a.m., on a train, on a plane, and on a rural Mexican bus (really!). My Harvard friend, meanwhile, did all of the above plus at least one in a walk-in freezer. That's why she's at Harvard and I'm not, I guess. Everybody has a story about how they would have done better if not for [some distraction] on test day. But we don't, and for that I'm thankful."

Don't Take the LSAT If You're Not Ready for It.

If you don't feel ready for the test, trust your instincts. You can withdraw up until 24 hours before the start time and nothing shows up on your LSAT record.

Show Up for the Test.

This means knowing *how* to show up.

Read the instructions. Know what you can and can't bring to the test. The watch you've been using for the past 6 months to time yourself during LSAT practice exams might be banned. Knowing beforehand will alleviate any such causes for major anxiety. Because some of these rules are crazy and strange and might rattle you, it is important to be informed.

Be prepared. Know how to find the room/testing center. Know where to park. Be prepared to be waiting an hour or two longer than expected; delays in getting started are common. If it is within your control, avoid sitting by the proctor (who will be—without exception—talkative and clueless) or by the door or other high traffic areas where panicking test takers will be running on their way to the bathroom.

It's OK to Take the LSAT Again.

No matter how well prepared you might feel for the LSAT, crazy things happen on test day. You may decide to cancel your score or wait for your score and then decide whether to retake the exam. Although the law schools will see all of your reported scores within a five-year period, they have every incentive to place the greatest weight on your highest score. This is what they report to the ABA and for rankings purposes. However, if you have a big difference between your scores, it might raise eyebrows so you will want to explain it in your application. (See

Chapter 9, "Explaining Your Weaknesses.") That weakness is overridden, however, by the fact that you hopefully received a higher score on the next exam. The other possible downsides of retaking the test are (1) the additional time spent studying; (2) cost of additional preparation/taking the exam again; (3) delay in getting your applications submitted/reviewed; and (4) the possibility that you might have to explain to a law school why your score decreased the second time.

Schools that say they average multiple LSAT scores are still inclined to take the higher score, especially if you provide a good explanation for why the first score shouldn't be held against you.

It's OK to Cancel an LSAT.

It may even show good judgment to cancel. You have six days after the LSAT to cancel a score in writing. It absolutely must be in writing, as per the instructions at www.LSAC.org. So, when should you cancel? If you completely screw up by leaving an entire section blank, mis-bubble the last six questions, or become violently ill in the middle of the exam, you should probably cancel. Other reasons for canceling may include significant (nearly unbearable) distractions in the testing center or if you already have an LSAT score that you believe is higher than what you likely earned on this test. Many of my clients know exactly that a certain game or reading passage threw them but that otherwise they performed within their anticipated range. I often tell them not to cancel in this situation (if it is their first time taking the LSAT) because it's likely that something will throw them on an LSAT exam. I've never had someone say to me that they got 8 hours of sleep the night before the test, took the perfect LSAT that hit all of their strengths, only had games they had seen before, had the best possible testing conditions with quiet neighbors and ran on schedule. All of these conditions have never occurred for any one person during any LSAT.

I always get a lot of phone calls on those four days a year when the LSAT is given and within an hour of when people are leaving the testing center— thank goodness they not all from the same time zone! Everyone wants to know whether they should cancel. I listen closely, let them vent, and then I tell them to call me in 24 or 48 hours. There is a reason you have six days to consider this decision—you should not be making this decision when you are stressed or exhausted. Go home after the test. Close the door. Refrain from logging onto a discussion forum to see what other people thought of the test. Watch a mindless movie (I would've said something with Bradley Cooper but then he went and got nominated for an Oscar—too heavy for post-LSAT coma inducement), eat junk food, and go to sleep. Wake up the next day, work out, and then really think. Then, if you still really aren't sure which section was the experimental or what you were supposed to do with the unicorn game (I made this up, don't go Google "unicorn LSAT game"), then start reading blogs by LSAT teachers and consider looking at the forums if you just can't resist. But don't make any decisions until you've slept on it. You don't get bonus points for canceling before anyone else. You get bonus points for good decision-making.

Here's the Truth about Very Low LSAT Scores

This is, unfortunately, the most popular topic on my blog and has been since I initially posted about it back in 2007. I am informally known as The Beacon of Hope for people who score under a 150 and for those who score in the low 150s but still hope to attend Top 30 law schools. While I do have testimonials on my website from people who fall into these categories and give me full credit for their acceptances, it should be understood that I practically hand-select these clients, knowing their lofty goals, because I see that there is something in their backgrounds that law schools will value. When someone with a history of LSAT scores in the low 140s calls me, I am very clear with them about whether their expectations are reasonable, and to be honest I turn away those who I feel are completely off base in terms of where they hope to attend given their credentials.

If your LSAT score is in the 140s or lower, you need to spend some time looking at the 25th percentile LSAT scores for the schools you were hoping to attend.[9]

If that number is more than 10 points higher than your LSAT score, please be realistic that your chances of admission are slim to none (especially if your GPA is also below the 25th percentile for that school). That's all there is to it— sorry, I don't sugarcoat things. [10]

You have three choices:

1. Retake the LSAT and improve your score by doing something differently than you did the first or second time. For NON-TRADITIONAL applicants, this can include reducing hours spent working, and for INTERNATIONAL applicants, it can include

---

[9] How do you find this information? https://officialguide.lsac.org/release/OfficialGuide_ Default.aspx

[10] I have had clients whose LSAT scores are in the high 140s admitted to Top 30 and even top 20 law schools. However, in absolutely every case there was both (1) a summa cum laude/valedictorian/3.9 academic background and (2) one or more significant obstacles overcome.

spending more time on English reading fluency, speed, and comprehension. Don't expect the same behavior to bring about different results. If you plan to retake the LSAT, do so only if you're willing to invest the time and money necessary to really improve the outcome. Think long and hard about whether you could improve your score by increased preparation time or changing your preparation methods, and whether you're willing to put in that effort. If so, then try again. If not, reconsider your goals. "Not going to law school is not the end of the world. In fact, it may turn out to be the best decision that you ever make," says Ronald Den Otter, pre-law advisor.

2. Be more flexible in your list of law schools by including schools that take people with your numbers. If a school never takes anyone with your numbers, then they won't take you—no matter how amazing your personal statement and letters of recommendation may be.

3. Re-think your plans to attend law school. After all, if you have a 2.3 GPA and a 138 LSAT, you, unfortunately, are very unlikely to make it through law school and then pass the bar exam when you graduate. So making this decision now, before you've invested three years and $150,000, could be the smartest thing you could do. This is especially true for those of you harboring a "dream" of becoming a lawyer but who do not have much practical experience in a legal environment and, therefore, may not understand the profession and its demands. I welcome people to fill out a form on my website for a free initial

consultation, and every year I hear from people who were academically dismissed from Thomas Cooley but "have always dreamed of being a lawyer."

Basic Guidelines for Low LSAT Scores:

- If you have a high 140s LSAT, a GPA at 3.5 or above, and no major arrests, discipline issues, etc., then if you apply to the right schools and submit the best possible application materials, you will probably be successful. If you have a mid-140s LSAT, a high GPA, and a history of accommodations that you were not awarded for the LSAT, you may also be successful with a persuasive application.

- If your grades are terrible and your LSAT score is under 150, I don't care if you have 20 years of experience as a paralegal and an MBA from the University of Phoenix, you are probably wasting your time applying to law school. Some mitigating factors include military service or coming from a significantly underprivileged background.

- If you have a 130s LSAT, you're not going to law school until you achieve a higher score. The end. (And, yes, I will answer this question exactly the same way no matter how many times or in how many variations it is posted as a comment on my blog.)

How do I Deal with Disabilities?

For those with disabilities, there is no waiver for the LSAT. However, Marni Lennon, Assistant Dean at the University of Miami School of Law, states,

> Students with disabilities have some strategic considerations when approaching this test. How and when

to disclose a disability is a very personal decision. Be sure to carefully consider the way in which your disability may impact your testing when making the decision whether to apply for accommodations. For some students, this means taking practice exams in accommodated and standard testing settings to assess impact. For others, it is immediately apparent that to take the test without accommodations would do a tremendous disservice to the applicant and not reflect the potential performance of that student. Should you seek accommodations, make sure that you have carefully reviewed the LSAC website regarding required documentation. It is terribly disheartening to see a student apply for accommodations, fail to supply all the requisite information, and then scramble with stress to get the rest of the documentation when all efforts should be on LSAT preparation. When applying for accommodations, be sure that your documentation not only adheres to the LSAC guidelines, but that the recommendations of the evaluating doctor are clear and specific, and correlate with underlying test scores, if applicable. On more than one occasion, students have sought accommodations and been denied because the requests are vague: 'Johnny would benefit from additional time.' Or, the form indicates 50% time but the accompanying psychoeducational report says the student should have a private room and has no mention of specific time, only noting that it may be helpful for overall performance. This will not fly! With medical conditions, it is important that the documentation indicate the present impact on a substantial life activity. For example, 'Stacy was in a car accident in 2007 and suffered internal injuries and broke her arm,' does not provide appropriate or useful information as to why accommodations are necessary now, or what they should be.

What about Conditional Acceptance Programs?

There are schools that will offer you the privilege of paying to take a summer course or two with the incentive that participants who earn a certain grade will be admitted to the fall entering class. These programs are sometimes referred to as "AAMPLE" (Alternative Admissions Model Program in Legal Education) programs. Sometimes conditional programs are online, and sometimes they are on campus. If your LSAT score isn't an accurate predictor of future academic success, this may be your best and only option. But there is no guarantee of acceptance, and before you commit to any programs ask about the number of people admitted during previous sessions and whether those people went on to graduate and/or were in good standing once enrolled as law students.[11]

---

[11] For a list of law schools with conditional acceptance programs, see http://www.lsac.org/jd/pdfs/conditional-admission-programs.pdf

CHAPTER 5

APPLICATION CHECKLIST

NOW that you know that you want to apply to law school, you need to create a checklist and timeline for yourself. An effective law school application cannot be thrown together in a week. Some of the things over which you maintain the least amount of control, such as letters of recommendation and transcripts, take the longest to obtain.

Here is a checklist to keep yourself on track:

1. *Register for CAS* (Credential Assembly Service). (How?) Transcripts and Letters of Recommendation must be sent through the CAS, and CAS then is responsible for sending these items (along with your Academic Summary Report (as per #6) and your LSAT score (as per #10) to each school where you end up applying (for a fee, as per #18, below).

2. *Get a professional sounding e-mail address* (e-mail names like2parTi and SexSImama probably need to be retired).

3. *Cultivate and ask for letters of recommendation* (at

least two and up to five). (See Chapter 6, "Letters of Recommendation.")

4. *Add recommender information to your CAS account.*

5. *Send transcripts to LSAC.* (See Chapter 3, "Your GPA.")

6. *Check your Academic Summary Report* (based on your transcripts) for errors/inconsistencies.

7. *Attend a law school forum or a campus recruiting event or visit your local law school(s).*

8. *Choose an LSAT date* (LSAC.org). (See Chapter 12, "The Application Timeline.")

9. *Select an LSAT prep method.* (See Chapter 4, "The LSAT.")

10. *Take the LSAT.*

11. *Collect fee waivers* (free applications)!

12. *Create and hone your resume.* (see Chapter 7, "Building Your Resume.")

13. *Write your personal statement.* (See Chapter 10, "The Personal Statement.")

14. *Create your draft addenda* (re: Character and Fitness (Chapter 9, "Explaining Your Weaknesses"); LSAT (Chapter 4, "The LSAT"), Grades (Chapter 3, "Your GPA"), or disability (Chapter 9, "Explaining Your Weaknesses").

15. *Create a list of schools, essay prompts, and requirements as per the application instructions and each school's website.* (See Chapter 14, "Choosing a Law School.")

16. *Write optional essays.* (See Chapter 11, "Writing Optional Essays.")

17. *Fill out applications online, then proofread them!* (See Chapter 13, "Filling Out Applications.")

18. *Pay for LSAC reports for each school and for the applications themselves.*

19. *Submit applications.*

CHAPTER 6

LETTERS OF RECOMMENDATION

What Is the Purpose of a Letter of Recommendation?

THE people writing your letters of recommendation are the only people who get to speak in your application other than you. This is the chance for someone to discuss your dedication, seriousness, intellectual curiosity, research and writing skills, communication skills, presentation skills, and teamwork and leadership in a way that you cannot without sounding arrogant. The best letters of recommendation are written by someone whom the reader will trust (credibility of credentials, but also credibility in terms of in what capacity the person supervised you).

Who Should I Ask to Write a Letter of Recommendation?

It's not who you know, it's how you know them and what meaningful things they can say about you to the law schools that's important.

The best letter of recommendation is the (strong) academic letter. A detailed letter from a professor outlining the rigor of the class(es) you took, how you excelled in them, describing your intellectual curiosity, writing and research skills, presentation skills and/or teamwork and problem-solving skills, is the best tool for law schools who are trying to ascertain whether you will make it through a rigorous law school curriculum. A strong academic letter can show you are more than just a strong GPA—that you actually care about what you study and contribute meaningfully and you are not interested only in grades. Likewise, if your undergraduate grades are lackluster, a strong academic letter can show a law school that you are more than your overall GPA shows. The letter can illustrate how you excel in classes that require the same skills you will need to succeed in law school, how you are a more serious student than your transcripts and/or resume may show, and it enables you to add a perspective about you from someone the law school will trust. "Keep in mind that if your recommender does not know you very well, it can be almost impossible for him or her to write you a decent letter even if he or she would like to help you," says Ronald Den Otter (who is a political science faculty member in addition to a pre-law advisor).

People who attend large public schools often have a hard time getting an academic letter, even if they were a good student. But remember, a teaching assistant who led a discussion group, who held office hours that you attended, and who graded your work can absolutely write a meaningful letter on your behalf. However, be sure the person will actually write you a strong letter. You can actually ask, "Do you feel you could write a strong letter on my behalf?" This will give people an out in the event that the teacher actually doesn't think you're as great as you think he thinks you are. "Most professors are more observant than you think they are. As such, keep in mind that how you act in class may not go unnoticed. When a professor sees you texting or using your laptop inappropriately, arriving late without a good excuse, or missing class, that behavior may make an unfavorable impression," says Den Otter.

The prestige of the professor is not nearly as important as what he or she can say about you that is meaningful.

What do I mean by "meaningful"?

- A description of the rigor of the course taken with the professor, including the kind of work that is required (essay exams, research papers, group projects, etc.).
- How you stood out, contributed to classroom discussion, sought out office hours—examples that show you are a serious student who is engaged in coursework, rather than simply showing up and doing the minimum required to get a certain grade.
- A comparison between you and other students the professor has taught who went on to law school (or even a certain level of law school).
- It is not helpful for a professor's letter of recommendation to recount achievements that he or she could not have known about you firsthand. Those achievements should be on your resume or from other parts of your application.

What If I Don't Have a Professor to Write a Letter?

For those of you out of school or who simply don't have a relationship with any of your professors, it is still possible to find a meaningful letter of recommendation.

Here are some ideas/suggestions for possible letter writers:

- *Supervisor:* Someone who is senior to you in a

professional environment and who has supervised you in tasks related to those that make for a successful law student and/or attorney is the next best bet. This person should address skills including managerial, leadership, communication, business experience, knowledge of processes of an organization, and an ability to work well with others and to solve problems proactively and responsibly. Examples of these skills are crucial to the letter's credibility. Of course, asking your supervisor can get sticky if you don't want your current employer to know you are applying to law school. If you feel comfortable having your supervisor write a letter for you, you should let him or her know that a letter of recommendation for law school is a different beast than the often-generic, overly broad professional reference. At the end of this chapter is a sample letter. Feel free to give it to your supervisor and to share the tips in this book with him or her.

- *Internship supervisor:* Consider this if and only if you really did something impressive during your internship. If you did a run-of-the-mill errand-running, coffee-grabbing, document-editing, phone-answering grunt-work internship, it's not likely to garner a very persuasive letter of recommendation. At the end of this chapter I have attached an example of a good internship letter of recommendation. (See more about internship letters, below, in "Who Should I Avoid Asking for a Letter of Recommendation?".)

- *Military service:* Your commanders actually write great letters of recommendation because they are detailed, usually in bullet point format, and very straightforward.

- *Professor from a graduate level course:* Consider taking a graduate level course and getting to know the professor. It might turn out that your interest in the course will establish a relationship with the professor and lead to obtaining a recent academic letter.

- P*rofessional at a non-profit organization:* If you have worked or volunteered your time at a non-profit, consider talking to one of the professional staff or managers to request a letter.

- *Professional you've worked closely with:* If you have owned your own business or have been a freelancer, consider asking a one of the professionals you have worked with (such as a lawyer or accountant) who can speak to your involvement with sophisticated issues.

Who Should I Avoid Asking for a Letter of Recommendation?

Family friends, the judge who plays tennis with your mother, or internship supervisors with nothing original to say are among the people NOT to ask for letters of recommendation. At all costs, AVOID the family friend letter—even when your parents swear their friends will write you fabulous letters. If you think you're an exception to this rule, you're not.

Why am I so insistent about this? It goes back to the *purpose* the letter serves in your application—to make your application stronger. The writer is the only person who gets to talk in your application other than YOU. Your letter writer must say things he or she knows about you from personal experience. These statements add credibility to the things you say about yourself in the rest of your application. The content of the letter must be relevant to your law school application; the person whose child you babysat—lawyer or not—is not in a position to speak to those qualities.

Even if your parents pressure you to ask their well-meaning, successful friends for letters, please say "Thanks, but no thanks." That nice judge who went to law school with your mom and who allowed you to "shadow" him for two hours cannot speak on your behalf. Why not? After all, you had an absolutely remarkable and interesting 20-minute conversation about law school and the practice of law during which you totally charmed and impressed him. Ok, think about what that letter might say:

> As a friend of Joey's mother for the past 22 years, I have heard stories of his progress. Between sets on the tennis court, she would tell me about his involvement with his fraternity and how proud she was of his performance in college. I have seen Joey many times in the last few years, during which I have seen that he is bright and polite. I understand he did well on his LSAT and that he has been active in his church. I am, therefore, confident he will make an outstanding law student.

BLECH. I know. Horrid. However, there may be a way to use this contact/offer of assistance. If you are applying to the law school this person attended, perhaps he could make a phone call or send an e-mail on your behalf to one of his contacts at the school. Or you could say, "Thank you so much, but I already have my requisite number of letters. Could I take you up on this offer if I am waitlisted? And perhaps, could I spend a week in your courtroom during my summer break? Or could you introduce me to any lawyers whom you think would be good mentors for me as I embark on my career?" (As I discuss in

The Law School Decision Game, networking is important. Turn this into an opportunity to start building your law career now!)

Likewise, avoid getting a letter from your internship supervisor unless you took the lead on a project or you acted in some way that was remarkable compared to the other interns at the organization. So many interns on Capitol Hill think their day is made because they have a two-sentence letter of recommendation from their Senator. Everyone knows all you did was conduct tours (unless you were the one to author Bruiser's Bill and introduce the snap cup[12]). If you were offered paid employment after the end of your internship, that's great, but it can probably be explained equally impressively on your resume, especially if your internship was in business, marketing, or investment banking and might leave people wondering why you would leave something so practical for law. If you worked in a law firm or legal office and you stayed beyond summer break and supervised other interns, etc., then I would make an exception to the "no internship letter" rule, especially if you are struggling to obtain academic letters.

How Should I Ask for a Letter of Recommendation?

- Give someone two to four weeks to write a letter. Professors may require even more lead time, especially during busy times of the academic year.
- Remember that the person is doing you a favor.
- If possible, ask in person rather than through e-mail.
- Go to office hours; don't interrupt the professor on the way in or out of class.
- Be straightforward.

---

[12] If you don't get this reference, you must be very, very young and you are probably a genius who is applying to law school at the age of 14.

I don't believe in the value of giving a professor your personal statement or resume to help write the letter because a letter of recommendation needs to add something new and shouldn't just read like a canned letter with phrases and items from your resume. A letter sounding like your resume will simply highlight the fact that the professor really doesn't know you at all and was a bit desperate for material. If a professor knows about your extracurricular activities firsthand (as advisor to a particular organization) or knows your work experience (because he recommended you for a particular job on your resume and/or discussed your experiences in a mentor capacity), then he or she can incorporate these items into a letter of recommendation with credibility. Instead of giving the professor your resume, give him or her bullet point reminders of the work you did in class.

If a professor seems lukewarm or less than enthusiastic about writing a letter or asks you to jump through hoops before he or she will agree to write the letter, this is a good indication that it might not be a strong letter. Remember, quality over quantity.

What Can I Do While Still in College to Make Sure I Get Good Letters of Recommendation?

Get to know your professors/letter writers. Don't just show up one day (or worse, send a random e-mail) and ask them to spend time writing letters of recommendation. Cultivate these letters through visits, coffee chats, intellectual discussions, and seeking advice about your goals and future career. And, of course, taking the class seriously helps, too! If you are in college, visit professors during office hours, try to take more than one class with at least two professors, and offer to help a professor with his or her research interests.

How Many Letters of Recommendation Do I Need?

LSAC will hold up to five letters for up to five years. I'd rather have only two letters where both are strong, than three letters where the third is less than stellar.

What Should I Do If They Ask Me to Write My Own Letter of Recommendation?

If someone asks you to prepare a letter of recommendation for his or her signature, do not freak out. This is fairly standard practice in the professional world.

Here's a brief outline of how to approach writing it yourself:

- Paragraph 1: Outline the writer's experience to build his or her credibility. Provide facts demonstrating the context in which the writer knows you, including supervisory role and the length of time the writer has known you.
- Paragraph 2: Provide an overview of your accomplishments and duties.
- Paragraphs 3 to 5: Use factual examples of certain characteristics you would like to highlight. Consider including a time you solved a problem in a professional and diplomatic way, an instance in which you demonstrated your writing skills, and/or your willingness to go above and beyond the call of duty. For example, instead of just stating you have communication skills, give examples of letters or materials you

created that were used for internal or external matters. Another valuable example would be detailing the time you were selected to be part of a more senior team and earned the respect of co-workers and/or senior managers.

- Conclusion: State the qualities you bring to law school and why the person highly recommends you for law school admission, and that he or she is available to answer questions about your experience and candidacy.

Do I Need Targeted Letters of Recommendation?

There are only two reasons to get a letter that is targeted to a specific law school: (1) the school (aka Stanford Law) requires it; or (2) the person writing your letter has a specific connection to the particular law school. If (1) or (2) doesn't apply to you, then you will just use the designation for "General" letters.

What is an Evaluation and Do I Need One?

OK, it was a good idea. In theory. LSAC offers online evaluations where recommenders are asked to rank you in a series of skill sets and qualities. Online evaluations were meant to give more quantitative, specific feedback about candidates. However, it never caught on. No law school seems to require evaluations. And now that letters can be submitted electronically, there isn't even a time-saving element to the evaluation process. So, as of this printing, I'd say you can pretty much ignore evaluations unless you're applying to the University of Montana, Albany, or Detroit Mercy.[13]

---

[13] http://blueprintprep.com/lsatblog/law-school-admissions/which-law-schools-require-evaluations/

How Do Letters Get Sent to Each School?

When you submit each application, you will designate the letters that you wish to accompany it. It's OK if the letter hasn't been received yet at LSAC. Your application will still be submitted, and the letter will follow on receipt.

How Long Can Letters Stay on File at LSAC?

If you are in college or graduate school and even remotely considering applying to law school at some point, please go ahead and register for LSAC and get letters of recommendation that can be held for future use because it's unlikely that your professors will remember you even a few weeks beyond graduation. LSAC will hold them for five years. There is no need to update an academic letter after a year or two, but a work reference from a current employer should be brought current.

Should I Waive My Right to See the Letter?

Yes. This doesn't mean you've never seen it or that it won't be shown to you in the future. It simply means you won't sue LSAC or the law schools to see your letters. It adds credibility to the letter because it is assumed that people will be more candid if they know you will not ever lay eyes on its content.

A Sample Letter of Recommendation

To Whom It May Concern:

I am writing to support S.N.'s (Student's Name) application for law school. As her supervising attorney at South Brooklyn Legal Services this past summer, I can attest to S.N.'s outstanding research and writing skills as well as her passion for legal services work. Even as an intern, she was a tremendous asset to this office and made a real difference in the lives of the clients on whose cases she worked. As a law student at your university, I know she would contribute more of the same top quality work I saw from her this summer.

First, in my five years as an attorney in the housing law unit at this office, I can honestly say that I have never had a better experience working with any summer intern. With every assignment I gave her, I could trust that S. would approach the work conscientiously and diligently and would return with an exceptionally well-researched and well-written work product. In fact, toward the end of the summer, I left S. almost entirely on her own to handle a case involving wrongful termination of a client's Section 8 subsidy. S. met with the client to identify the problem and collect relevant documents from her, identified the claims involved, and drafted the federal court complaint and the brief in support of an order to show cause. Her understanding of the issues was so accurate, and her writing so clear, that I barely edited the papers before filing them in court.

Second, it is not only S.N.'s research and writing skills that are superb. I observed her interactions with clients in settings ranging from court appearances to office appointments to tenant association meetings. Without exception, S. was compassionate, patient, and professional. Likewise, she was articulate and confident in her interactions with opposing counsel in court.

Finally, I have met very few law students—and indeed, few young attorneys—who are as mature as S. is in their commitment to legal representation for the poor. She truly believes in the importance of the work and knows how to translate that belief into high quality advocacy. The attorneys at South Brooklyn Legal Services, as well as our clients, benefited enormously from S.N.'s dedication this past summer. We will be thrilled if she returns to this office as an intern or attorney in the future.

My direct line is ( ) _____ -_____. Please feel free to call if I can be of any further assistance.

Yours truly,

Attorney's Name

Senior Staff Attorney Housing Law Unit

CHAPTER 7

BUILDING YOUR RESUME

Do I Need a Resume with My Law School Applications?

YES. I view the resume as the greatest opportunity to share with the law school how you have spent your time. If you do a great job on your resume, it frees up your personal statement to cover things that are more interesting and thoughtful about you. Although applications may have you fill in basic information about jobs and activities, there is no room on applications to extrapolate. It's one thing merely to state you were Vice President of your fraternity. However, it adds a new dimension to explain that as Vice President of Standards and Risk Management you had to handle the forced resignation of a fellow officer over some indiscretion, or as Treasurer you oversaw bringing the chapter out of debt and into a $10,000 surplus. The resume is what allows you to do this effectively.

This is your chance to show leadership and share the extent to which you self-financed your education, any cultural or volunteer activities, language proficiencies, athletic talents, or experiences living in another country. Give details of your work experiences during college and show, for example, what your job as an Office Manager or Sales Associate really entailed and what you accomplished in each role.

What Are Some Basic Rules of Resume Writing?

- Avoid referring to yourself in the first person.
- Use action words at the beginning of your descriptions.
- Use past tense to describe things you did in the past and present tense to describe current duties.
- It's OK to go onto a second page IF you're doing it because of the substance and not because of the design you are using.
- Do NOT include high school. Your high school honors, athletics, and awards got you into college; now you need to stand on your accomplishments post-college.

I know you might be thinking, "The *no high school rule* doesn't apply to me because I was high school valedictorian/ an Eagle Scout/captain of the football team/community service awardee. To consider yourself special in this regard is a big mistake. Emphasizing high school often unwittingly highlights youth ("she was in high school three years ago?"), immaturity ("she thinks *this* is important?"), lackluster college performance ("she didn't do so well once she moved out from the under the watchful eye of mommy and daddy"), and privilege ("she went to *that* high school?"). Perhaps I'm being cruel, but this is absolutely necessary to help you create an effective resume.

Since you are an aspiring lawyer, you should know that every rule has an exception. Even I have made exceptions for those clients whose high school accomplishments add context to their later achievements.

Examples of exceptions are:

- Playing as a member of a professional symphony at age 16.
- Competing in Olympic-level events.
- Moving to the United States while in high school and learning English as a second language as a teenager and still graduating from high school with honors.
- Attending a fancy prep school on full scholarship and your socio-economic circumstances would have otherwise prevented your attendance.
- International students who attended boarding school in the United States or in another English-speaking country may add this to their resumes to demonstrate experience studying in the English language.

How Should I Organize My Resume?

Generally, include the sections that apply to you. The main section headings for your resume may include:

- Education
- Experience
- Activities
- Community Service
- Accomplishments
- Skills
- Travel
- Interests

Education:

This section should include all of your degree institutions

and certificates, but does not need to include every school you ever attended if you only attended for a summer, etc. (You may include Study Abroad under this heading.) This section comes first because you are applying for professional school, and this is what law schools care about the most. If you've been out of school for ten or more years and your undergraduate history is nothing special, I might be okay with Education following Experience. However, in this case, the professional experience should be very impressive and not simply ten years' worth of twenty different administrative positions.

The Education section should include, in reverse chronological order, the schools you have attended since high school graduation. Only in very rare circumstances should you include high school. One example was for my client who was applying to the University of Texas and she was trying to show ties to Texas that would not have otherwise been evident from other aspects of her background (since she attended college in New York City).

Include:
- Proper Name of Degree, Date Conferred or Anticipated
- Formal Name of University, City, State
- Major/Minor Information
- GPA (if over 3.0)

Honors: Include graduation honors, thesis topic, the number of semesters on Dean's List, honor society memberships, and scholarships and awards received.

Extracurricular Activities: You should list each activity in reverse chronological order and include your role in the organization, the extent of your involvement, dates of involvement, and any particular accomplishments. If you have a number of things in this category, you should probably separate this out from the Education section.

Experience

You should include all jobs and internships post-high school. It can be broken up into different headings, such as College Work Experience and Professional Experience, or Legal Experience and Teaching Experience, as appropriate for your background.

This section should include all jobs because:

- You are trying to account for your time.
- There's no shame in showing a law school you're not above a little grunt work.
- These jobs add context to your grades and other achievements, even helping to explain why you had a hard time with grades during a semester when you had to work full time.
- Demonstrates time management skills.
- Shows you weren't a recluse and that you had to deal with other people in a stressful or fast-paced environment.
- Unglamorous or "menial" jobs build character and demonstrate a lack of elitism.

Exceptions to the "all jobs" rule are rare but here are a few:

- If you made a living as a professional gambler, you might have second thoughts about sharing it. However, it can add character and an interesting aspect to your application. One of my clients, who is graduating from a top law school, took this approach with her application and it showed savvy and sophistication and smarts.
- Job hopping: Jobs you held for a month probably shouldn't be listed by themselves.

When describing each job, include something specific rather than generalities (e.g., "learned valuable business skills"). For example, instead of "Sold and marketed homes," try "Assisted in the sale of four homes, resulting in more than $3 Million in sales.

Avoid "over-selling." Everyone knows what a legal assistant does, and it sounds disingenuous to write that you were drafting motions to dismiss and single-handedly taking cases to trial. Likewise, a customer service representative at the Gap or a barista at Starbucks does not need to go crazy with describing duties. The reader can use his imagination.

Activities

If you were involved in a number of activities, then you should make this a separate section with more detail than in the Education section. You should include college and post-college extracurricular activities and a description of the extent of your involvement in each. List each activity in reverse chronological order and include your role in the organization, the extent of your involvement, dates of involvement, and any particular accomplishments.

Here are some tips:

- Don't refer to yourself as a "Leader" unless you held a series of indisputable leadership positions. It can sound arrogant and misguided to say you are a "leader" because you were the scholarship chair of a service fraternity.

- If you joined the pre-law society or Phi Alpha Delta your last year in school, it will look like obvious resume-filler. State that you participated meaningfully, perhaps by saying: "Attended weekly events, helped coordinate law school panel events each semester, and actively worked with prelaw advisors and professors to create prelaw programming on campus."

- Don't assume everyone knows what the "Blue Key Society" is, but do assume everyone knows what the "Golden Key Honour Society" is, and please spell it correctly because everyone knows how it should be spelled.

- Detail duties, responsibilities, and accomplishments. The point of sharing activities on your resume is to demonstrate your interests and passions and to show that you seriously committed yourself to each. Therefore, stating your duties and accomplishments and the hours you spent devoted to the activity will make the resume more meaningful. It's one thing to list, "Member, ABC" and it's another to list, "Member, ABC (2008—2012), actively involved in recruiting 12 new members in 2009 and 22 in 2010

as member of the recruiting committee. 2 hours/
week." Much more impressive and meaningful, right?

- If you've only done one or two community service
events, and/or if your only community service activities have been through a Greek organization, do not
have a separate section for Community Service. If you
have multiple examples, then include these involvements under Community Service.

- Do not include anything you only did for a day, like
showing up for Relay for Life.

- For NON-TRADITIONAL applicants, you can
list professional organizations, sitting on non-profit
boards, canvassing for elections, and volunteering at
your child's school. Dig deep for ideas; don't assume
you have nothing worth including. Members of the
military should include their volunteer services in the
communities where they were serving.

Community Service

Include volunteer activities that were meaningful, and
describe the organizations and your duties and contributions
just as you would any other activity or job. If your only community service experience was through a Greek organization,
leave it off your resume. It can look overblown to describe it
separately. Likewise, anything you did only for an afternoon is
not significant enough to be resume-worthy.

Travel

Stick with international travel. Seeing the world is a good
thing. Showing law schools you've seen the world is a good
thing. When can it be a bad thing? When it sounds more like

you come from a privileged family and you tagged along with your parents to Turks and Caicos and Tahiti.

Interests

You can include anything you consider significant, even if it demonstrates religious or political affiliation.

Accomplishments

Here you can include running marathons, belt status for martial arts, published articles, etc.

Skills

Include languages, musical abilities, computer languages, etc. This section helps to show you are well rounded in ways that your transcripts, letters of recommendation, and other application materials may not reflect. Do not include computer skills such as "Internet Research and Microsoft Office." These are now simply life skills and are not exceptional in any way. If you have been a legal secretary and you are trying to show familiarity with billing and calendaring software, just leave it off your resume. It won't impress anyone, and it will be understood from your job description. If you have computer programming skills or other technical skills, they can be included.

Only include language skills if you would feel comfortable with an admission counselor calling you and speaking in that language. Also, don't include fluency in English; I should hope that's a given. If you list another language, state how you garnered a level of fluency in that language. Was it spoken in your home? Did you live abroad? Did you study it in high school and college?

You may have noticed three common headings missing from the list: Summary of Qualifications, Objectives, and Relevant

Coursework. Only include a Summary if you have been working for more than five years in multiple positions, and if you are trying to pull together experiences that seem unrelated. For example, if you are trying to explain that although you've worked in both the pharmaceutical and the public relations industries, you were managing budgets and employees in both settings. If you decide to incorporate this section, it should include concrete statements of facts rather than generalities such as "Extensive history of providing excellent customer service." These statements are really only credible when someone else is saying them; on your resume for law school, they feel like fluff.

Do NOT include an Objectives section. Please. Your objective is to get into the law school you are applying to. That's it. So don't state the obvious.

It's not necessary to list Relevant Coursework because your transcripts are attached to your application. Besides, nearly all courses are "relevant" to law school since the law interacts with pretty much everything from Engineering to International Relations to Art (copyright protection).

How Should I Build My Experiences on My Resume?

A lot of people ask me what they can do to improve their selection of jobs/activities to round out their resumes before applying to law school. If you still have at least six months before applying to law school, make an honest assessment of your experiences now that you've seen them on paper. Do your interests seem all over the map? Are all of your involvements surface-level? Is there anything you can do this year to show growth in a particular existing interest, such as taking on a bigger role within a group or volunteer effort? Are you lacking real-world experience? Can you take on a part-time job? If you're afraid you don't look like a very serious person, can you become a research assistant or teaching assistant for a professor that would highlight a sincere academic interest and ability? If you've been working in one (non-law related) profession for years, is there a volunteer activity you could undertake that would show a more clear affinity for studying and practicing law? Take time for introspection; it's seldom harmful and neglecting to do so leads to laziness and an inflated sense of self. Be proactive about adding depth or breadth to your experiences.

CHAPTER 8

EVALUATING YOUR STRENGTHS

A S a law school admission consultant, I spend consider-able time and energy thinking about each of my client's strengths. Almost everyone has something, whether it's evident from their resumes and transcripts or not. Sometimes I have to get people to dig deep and think of themselves as a third party would; often we can't see the interesting parts of our own stories simply because they are our own. In this chapter's discussion of strengths and soft factors, we are leading up to the really big chapter—the Personal Statement (Chapter 10). Until you've really thought about your strengths, you're not ready to think about what to write in your personal statement. (This is the same as dealing with your weaknesses, by the way, because you will need to know what you have to counteract for your personal statement to be effective.)

What Are Soft Factors?

Anything outside of your LSAC Cumulative GPA and LSAT score is considered a "soft" factor in the admissions process. The biggest problem I see is that people overestimate the value of their soft factors. An internship with your Congress member or a district attorney's office is not going to "wow" anyone. It's nice, but it's fairly standard. A summer studying abroad (especially in an English-speaking country) is not earth-shattering either.

Here are examples of impressive soft factors (juxtaposed with people who *say* they have good soft factors):

Student Activities and Leadership

Being a member of Phi Alpha Delta is nice and shows you've been interested in law (particularly if you did not join recently in order to add it to your resume), but law schools will always, without question, prefer to see in-depth leadership and exploration of your passions over resume fillers that you think sound good for a law school applicant. Whether it's a cultural organization, student government, athletics, or volunteerism, you need to demonstrate leadership, growth, and dedication in your involvements rather than simply collecting memberships in a number of different groups. If you use your time in college to explore things that really interest you, no matter how prestigious you feel they look to others, law schools will take notice.

If you are going to focus your undergraduate commitments in a Greek organization, then use this time to develop skills. For example, as treasurer or house manager you would handle real responsibilities, address conflicts, and gain practical skills. Do not overstate your experiences—all fraternities have public service so don't give yourself credit for great volunteerism unless you've really gone above and beyond to contribute to and/or lead your organization's philanthropic efforts.

Athletics

Being a Division 1 (or III for that matter) athlete during college shows dedication and time management, and a host of other skills. If you kept your grades up while pursuing athletics, law schools are going to be impressed. If you were heavily involved in a club sport, this can also be a plus factor in your application. A lot of people start out as college athletes and do not stick with it either because they are injured, or the pressure gets to them, or their grades suffer, or they do not get to play in games as much as they would like. I've read a lot of injured athlete stories. If you really used this experience as a turnaround and can truly demonstrate you picked yourself back up, applied your newfound time to your academics (and perhaps to apply your passions toward another extracurricular endeavor), then you can use this as a positive. However, if you haven't participated in your sport for a couple of years and you floundered after, then please do not write a personal statement about being an athlete. I don't want you to sound like a has-been.

If you are a NON-TRADITIONAL applicant with some time having passed since your college years, showing your involvement in sports at the time can be a way to distance yourself from your academic record (assuming it's lackluster). However, this probably shouldn't be addressed in your personal statement; it's more appropriate for an explanation of weaknesses. (See Chapter 9, "Explaining Your Weaknesses.")

International Experience

Study abroad is really common, so by itself I do not consider it a plus factor in your application—especially if you went to a popular American tourist destination (London, Melbourne, Italy, Spain, etc.). If you traveled somewhere really exciting or interesting then this might be more of a source of interest in your application. If you really explored a language and did an immersion program, there is value in that. Foreign language fluency is valued by law schools, absolutely. Volunteering in an impoverished country is going to be more eye-opening than spending your parents' money attending sporting events and seeing West End shows (especially since study abroad grades don't factor into your transcript evaluations by LSAC).

However, if you lived abroad during a formative period in your life, chose to do so as an adult, became fluent in another language, and gained meaningful insight into another culture, then this is interesting and persuasive in a law school application. The United States is a microcosm of people from different backgrounds, nationalities, and cultures. Your ability to work within this environment is seen as a plus factor in your application.

INTERNATIONAL students often wonder how much they count as being "diverse." Honestly, of course, you are diverse. You bring something interesting and different to the equation. If you received a scholarship to boarding school, if you sought to improve your own circumstances even without parents pushing you, this is all impressive and counts as overcoming obstacles. I've had an increasing number of international students as clients in recent years and these questions come up frequently, particularly as people decide whether to write a diversity statement. (See "Writing Optional Essays," Chapter 11.)

Work Experience

Let me start by going on a tangent about what lawyers really need to be good at: most of you will be in business as a lawyer. Having business skills, knowing how to make a profit, being good with people—this is all essential to success as a lawyer. Therefore, demonstrating that you have already begun to develop these skills is a huge plus in your application. Having an understanding of how the world works, not being afraid of grunt work, and a willingness (eagerness!) to work hard are all huge plus factors (when balanced with intellectual/academic abilities) in your law school application.

Working during college shows financial self-reliance and multi-tasking ability. For NON-TRADITIONAL applicants, professional work experience takes this even further. I've had clients with 20+ years as a paralegal, others who have run businesses, and even been dentists, philanthropists, actors, dancers, aestheticians, and poker players. In these cases, you need to show why law school makes sense for you at this time in your life and that you know what you're getting yourself into. It can also show a willingness to put in a crazy amount of hours (paralegal), to do lowly tasks to pursue a discipline (actors); to spend hours and hours practicing and fine tuning a craft (dance); to have a capacity for building a practice (dentist); to have a passion for helping others (philanthropist); to possess a practical sense of what has to be done to feed yourself and/or a family (aesthetician); to fully engage a sophisticated mind and have the ability to put yourself out there (poker player).

Internships

Internships are, in fact, different from work experiences. You may or may not have been paid (if you were, you should say so on your resume). These opportunities also vary greatly in terms of the exposure they offer to real office operations and substantive decision-making. Many people (OK, usually their parents) assume that fancy-sounding internships with

District Attorneys or Congress people or law firms are incredibly impressive. During the free initial consultation I offer for my law school admission consulting services, parents will often call and will often start by telling me that their adult child has had "great internships." These invariably include things like "Semester in DC" programs, interning with a member of Congress (which really just means answering calls and giving tours), or something along these lines. Then they proceed to tell me that the Congress person will be writing their "child" a fabulous letter of recommendation. Of course it's good to have internships, but it's better to do something you're really passionate about, something different, off the beaten path. Or, conversely, to come back to the same job more than once to show you are handling increased responsibility and are seen as a more permanent member of the professional team rather than another pre-law student passing through the office. If you have had two or three internships in quasi-related fields, it shows that you are really exploring a potential career. I like to see that. If you've had two or three internships in totally unrelated fields (public relations, sports, journalism, law, etc.) then it just looks like you don't know what you want to do—you are lacking direction and haven't found your stride yet.

Diversity

Before you read this section, take a deep breath. Some of you do not bring diversity to the table. You need to be ok with this. You can't worry about being at a disadvantage in the law school admission process because you haven't been disadvantaged in your life. I promise you, diversity alone won't get someone with a 2.3 and 140 LSAT into law school instead of you. And I'm not going to waste time arguing about whether affirmative action is fair; I'm not going to change your mind, and I promise you aren't going to change mine. So let's just stay focused on what you need to know for law school applications.

What counts as diversity? Here is the clear winner: Overcoming significant disadvantage, usually socio-economic, as the child of immigrants, growing up in subsidized housing and/or using food stamps, attending schools where a significant portion of the population did not come from English-speaking homes, growing up in a single-parent family, and overcoming barriers and disabilities (including abuse, poverty, and tragedy). The key, however, is in *overcoming* the circumstances. You won't get into law school with a series of excuses in your personal statement making your disadvantages very clear but not your ability to overcome them. After all, what's impressive is that you got yourself that degree despite lack of parental support, learned English as a teenager, and/or contributed to your family's finances while putting yourself through college, and as a result, have a valuable perspective—one that will help you as an attorney relate to (perhaps similarly-situated) clients.

Being fluent in a language other than English is very helpful for an attorney given the diverse population of our country and the globalization of our daily lives. Understanding what it feels like to be a minority or someone who has been ostracized (for example, coming of age in post 9/11 America as a Muslim or Pakistani or Sikh or living in the Bible Belt and being gay) is another way of demonstrating diversity. For more on this, please see the discussion of diversity statements in Chapter 11, "Writing Optional Essays."

CHAPTER 9

EXPLAINING YOUR WEAKNESSES

When and How Should I Explain a Weakness in My Application?

THERE are basically two types of weaknesses that may be explained in a law school application: mandatory and contextual. *Mandatory* includes character and fitness questions such as criminal record, infractions, disciplinary infractions, gaps in your education, etc.); *contextual* is meant to provide context/explanations/background to your achievements (LSAT, GPA, disability explanation, etc.). Your explanation of these issues in your application is typically referred to as an "Addendum" to your application.

General Rules about Addenda

They should be brief factual statements; this is not the time for narrative devices or histrionics. This is the time when you are most like a lawyer: State your facts, provide an argument for why this issue won't plague you during law school or in your legal career, and get out. Sob stories don't work here. The following discussion includes some of the topics that arise most often in addenda.

How Do I Explain My Lackluster Grades?

The best excuses for a poor GPA are:

o   Working your way through school.
o   Changing from a science-based major (from pre-med to pre-law).
o   Personal or family trauma.
o   Participation in intercollegiate athletics.
o   Undiagnosed or untreated disability and/or medical condition.

Provide Evidence: The best way to show that your GPA should not be used to judge your potential to compete in law school is to provide evidence. For example:

• "For my first two years of college, I worked 35 hours per week as a waitress to support myself and my daughter. After I got married, in the fall of 2007, I no longer needed to work more than 15 hours per week. Beginning that semester and continuing through the rest of college and through my master's degree program, my GPA never fell below a 3.5 and I earned Dean's List honors during my last three semesters of college." (This shows that the circumstances that prevented your early dismal performance have been overcome, and you have proof that you are capable of performing at a higher level than your early grades would indicate.)

• "As a college freshman, I felt great pressure to follow in my parents' footsteps by becoming a mechanical engineer. However, I struggled in the prerequisite courses because I was not interested in the topics. When I took my first political science class, I felt sincerely engaged in the work and was rewarded with my first "A" grade in college. After I changed my major to political science, my GPA stayed above a 3.6."

- "My grades dropped in my junior year because (my father died/I had mononucleosis/my parents lost their jobs). For the next two years, I was commuting home often to help my family/get medical treatment/attend rehab. Therefore, my transcripts do not accurately reflect my academic promise. However, [the problem has now been resolved by X] and these issues will not continue to inhibit my academic performance in law school."

- "For the first three years of college, I spent X hours/week training, practicing, and traveling as a member of the Division 1 tennis team. During a match in March 2010, I injured my shoulder. After that, I was unable to play tennis, and my time was spent in physical therapy. I struggled with depression and motivation after this change in my life, but finally rallied to concentrate on school during my last semester. In the spring of 2012, I earned a 3.7 GPA while taking three 400-level classes, which demonstrates my academic success when I am able to focus on school (which I plan to do in law school)."

The most common/less powerful excuses for your lackluster GPA:

If you were a typical 18 year-old living away from home for the first time, who was more interested in partying and video games than attending classes, the good news is that you are in good company. Perhaps not for Top 10 schools—I'll be very honest here—but if you got your act together, demonstrating maturity and growth then you'll have a story that works. Did you get a job that showed a level of dedication not evident in your grades? Get involved in a meaningful activity? Those things can help, but it's still a hard hurdle to overcome in an addendum, and it is very important for those of you who fall into this category to draft a really effective addendum. You may choose instead to showcase your strengths in your personal statement and not try to write an addendum that simply says, "I wish I hadn't partied so hard in college…."

NON-TRADITIONAL applicants have an easier time overcoming this issue. Did you return to school (for more college or for a graduate degree) later and succeed? Serve in the military? Are you successful in a profession? Have more than 5 years passed since you graduated from college? Are you now a parent? Demonstrate that you bring an understanding of how the real world works, that you are an adult now, and that you understand what it takes to succeed in the things that really matter, that you know how to prioritize your life, and that you make good decisions. Do not do this by using these phrases— do it by establishing credibility through the facts.

What If I Was on Academic Probation?

This is not discretionary—you have to tell the schools if you've been on academic probation. For most schools, this means you had a GPA at or under 2.0. This addendum can be combined with another GPA-related addendum.

What If I Took Time Off from School?

This is not discretionary. Schools ask on their applications whether you took any time off during your educational career. Explain whether you withdrew, took a leave of absence, or decided not to attend, and provide a reason. You need to include dates and what you did during the gap time. This is often combined with an academic probation explanation and/or a lack of maturity explanation.

What If I Have to Check "YES" on a Character and Fitness Question?

Have you ever been charged with a crime?

The most common affirmative responses to this question are due to Driving Under the Influence, use of a fake ID, minor in possession citations, and shoplifting. Will these types of issues keep you from being admitted to law school? The keys to a persuasive explanation are *Recency* and *Severity*. Is it a one-time incident, or is there a pattern that might show substance abuse problems and/or lack of judgment? This is where recency comes into play. If you've had a DUI and a possession arrest within the last year, it's going to be hard to show that you've had time to take your life seriously and turn things around. However, if you have one issue on your record, and it was from when you were 18 and you've been clean since, then it probably won't continue to plague you. That being said, you still have to report it.

DO NOT LIE: You are being tested on candor—the worst thing you can do is lie on your application, get caught in the lie after spending $100,000 or more on your law degree, and not be able to practice law because you were found to be untruthful on your law school or bar application (when trying to be licensed to practice law). Better to own up to it.

Here's an example:

> On June 12, 2009, when I was twenty years old, I was seen by a police officer as I was vomiting in a park. He approached me and stated that he smelled alcohol and asked for my identification. Using poor judgment as a result of the alcohol, I handed the officer my friend's identification card. He asked me if this was really mine, and I immediately owned to the fact that it was not and I apologized. I was fully cooperative with the officer and was charged with underage drinking and possession of a fake ID. I went to court on August 14, 2009, and because the officer did not appear, the charges were dismissed. This incident served as a wake-up call for me: I now use better judgment with alcohol and have spoken to my fraternity about the dangers of underage drinking. In the four years since this incident, I have not had any other violations of law and am in the process of having the charges expunged. I will update my application when this has occurred.

What If I Had an Honor Code Violation?

These are the incidents that are most dicey. For obvious reasons, law schools hold law students and lawyers to a high standard of ethical conduct. You will have to take a course and a separate exam about professional ethics to practice law. You will then have a continuing obligation to take professional credits in the subject once you are a practicing attorney. So, if you have anything in your background where your ethics have been called into question, you need to be sitting up straight when you approach the moral character and fitness questions.

Every law school will inquire about incidents involving academic dishonesty. This includes plagiarism, cheating accusations, or anything along these lines that usually results in a student conduct/honor council proceeding and/or action, or a failing grade as punishment for an academic conduct issue. To be honest, this is often something that comes into play with INTERNATIONAL STUDENTS when they first come to study in the United States. They are not necessarily aware that they need to cite source materials or how to do it. If this is the case and you made an honest (cultural) mistake and never had any incidents after one where you learned this lesson, you will need to explain it, of course, but it may not detract significantly from your applications. I had a client in this situation who went on to earn very high grades after an occurrence of this sort and although his LSAT score was in the low 150s, he was admitted to several Top 50, and even a Top 25, law school with this on his record.

If your ethical incident did not fall into this category, my advice is to be honest about it; show that you have taken it seriously and that it has served as a learning experience/turning point for you. Remember to include dates, exact charges, and the process, etc. It's very important that you don't sound bitter, for example, blaming the professor or administration. Taking responsibility is essential to retaining your credibility. Otherwise, you risk sounding like a complaining problem child.

I might also suggest that you obtain paperwork and/or a letter from the Dean of Students who oversaw the conduct charge/incident to add credibility to your statement showing that you have turned yourself around, you completed everything that was asked of you, and you are graduating in good standing. A statement of this type is sometimes referred to as a Dean's Certification or Dean's Letter.

What If I Have a Disciplinary Incident?

Did you smoke pot in the dorms? Throw a party that was too loud? Toss donuts off the balcony as part of a fraternity stunt? Yeah, I've heard it all before. You're entitled to a youthful indiscretion or two, really. I know there are some readers who won't take this advice, but the best thing you can do is report these incidents honestly. Don't over blow them (e.g., my girlfriend put the drink in my hand right before the cops came and I am so terribly sorry and I've gone to church every Sunday ever since and I only drink one beer at parties now).

Simply report them candidly, include the relevant details (and only the relevant details), and get out.

Here's an example:

> In May of my sophomore year of college, after final exams were complete, three friends and I decided to climb to the roof of our dorm and flash the onlookers as part of our year-end celebration. Unfortunately, one of the witnesses was the Dean of Engineering, who immediately reported to our dorm supervisor that four girls matching our description were topless on the roof. As we came out of the stairwell, the dorm supervisor pulled us aside and wrote us up for inappropriate conduct. We had to clean trash out of dorm rooms that had already been abandoned for the semester as our punishment. After we did this, our written disciplinary record was torn up. This incident is incredibly embarrassing and not at all indicative of how I have conducted myself in the last three years.

Do I Really Have to Report Speeding Tickets?

Most law schools exclude traffic violations from things that have to be reported under the Character and Fitness section of the application, but a few specifically include them. Please do not panic. If you can't remember the date or exact fine of the speeding ticket you got ten years ago, just approximate and provide the information to the best of your knowledge. If you recall the tickets, include the date, exact name of the citation, any pertinent details, that you paid the fine, that it was removed from your record, etc. This is pretty basic stuff and unless you led police on a high-speed chase, this isn't the kind of thing that will have a negative impact on your application.

LSAT Explanations

The LSAT is the only objective piece of your law school application. It is the only way you will be judged exactly equally with everyone else; it's hard to be subjective about the results of a test that everyone takes under the same conditions.

However, there are some circumstances when subjective value can be added, and it can work in your favor if you do it well.

Do I have to explain multiple LSAT Scores? When do you need to explain multiple LSAT scores and when can you leave it alone?

Leave it alone IF:

- You took it twice and the scores are within 3 points from each other.
- You simply have one cancellation and one score that you are sticking with.

Explain it IF:

- You think your pattern looks weird, like taking the LSAT three times and getting the exact same (or close) score every time. Explain why you kept trying. What did you expect to be different the second or third time?

- You had a significant score increase. Why? Additional preparation? A bad test day? Being sick the day you took the test the first time? Distractions in the test center? A specific reason helps.

Here are some examples:

Increase Due to Additional Preparation:

When I took the LSAT in October 2012 and received a 152, I realized I had not put in the effort required to perform to my abilities on the test. This served as a wake-up call for me and I set aside additional time for preparation. I decided to take a year off after college so that I could concentrate on the law school application process more fully. My October 2013 LSAT score of 164 is the result of my additional preparation and re-prioritizing, and is therefore a better example of my abilities.

Dip in Scores:

My first LSAT score (166 in December 2012) was three points lower than my average score on timed practice exams. Therefore, I decided to retake the LSAT in February 2013. However, I got the flu three days before the exam and was still recovering when I took the test. I was still feeling weak. In hindsight, I exercised bad judgment by not canceling my score. When I saw my score (162), I felt that I had to redeem myself. Therefore, I took the June 2013 LSAT. Before the test, I was scoring in the 167-171 range on timed practice tests. Unfortunately, I received a 165 on the test. However, my persistence in continuing to try to reach my goals is evidence of my desire to excel.

Distraction in Test Center:

Although I was consistently scoring in the mid-150s on timed practice exams, I received a 148 on the October 2013 LSAT. Unfortunately, I was seated by the front desk and found myself very distracted by talking and foot traffic. My December 2013 score (154) was not inhibited by these distractions and is a better representation of my abilities.

What If I'm Not a Good Standardized Test Taker?

If you have never taken a standardized test before (for example, if you attended community college and then transferred to a four-year university) or (for NON-TRADITIONAL applicants) if it has been a very long time since you took a standardized exam, then this is something that should be pointed out in an addendum.

Likewise, if you were working full-time and/or devoted to family responsibilities while studying for the LSAT, you should share that information in an addendum. It helps to give the reader a context for your score that he or she might not otherwise be aware of.

If you have a history of underperformance on standardized tests, you should explain this. The issue is, when do you have a history of underperformance and when do you simply WISH you had done better on the test?

If you have a score on the LSAT that is comparable to your SAT or ACT score in terms of percentile and that score was low for your entering class in college, you performed superbly in comparison to your peers. This helps prove that you have a history of underperformance on standardized tests because it shows that when you competed against people who received higher standardized test scores, you excelled. This argument does not work, however, if your grades in college were mediocre. It just isn't as compelling to say, "Although my SAT score was below the 50th percentile for my entering class at Cornell, my grades placed me in the top 50 percent of my class." It is, however, compelling to say, "Although my SAT score was in the bottom 10 percent of my freshman class at Cornell, I earned a 3.89 GPA there, placing me in the top 5 percent of my class. Therefore, the SAT failed to predict my academic performance. Likewise, my LSAT score of

162 is not a good indicator of how I will perform at a law school where the 25th percentile LSAT score is 167."

If you simply really want to go to a Top 10 school (despite your 3.3 at a good but not amazing university and a 161 LSAT), then consider whether an addendum is really appropriate. If your LSAT score is consistent with your SAT score, and your SAT score was mid-range for your college and your grades are mid-range at your college, it's very hard to make the argument that standardized tests fail to predict your academic performance.

If you come from an underprivileged background and you lacked the necessary support and resources to compete on standardized exams, this is absolutely worth sharing. This might include attending underprivileged schools, not having support at home, not being able to afford a prep course or tutoring, etc.

How Do I Explain a Learning Disability?

Every year, I hear from a lot of people who have documented learning disabilities but are refused accommodations on the LSAT. I won't waste your time by going on a tangent about the evils of LSAC, or why they refuse accommodations to so many people who have always received them, or anything about the constant flurry of lawsuits thrown at them after people are refused accommodations. It might be because your reports aren't from the right people, or because you perform in accordance with average test takers when you take tests without accommodations, or because you refused accommodations in completely different settings. I will simply say that if this happened to you, you are in very, very good company. So what can you do about it in terms of explaining it to law schools?

State the facts:

- Date of diagnoses (including if it was reaffirmed after the initial test date).
- Disability diagnosed. "Be specific. It helps the reviewer understand the link between the diagnosis and the test scores," advised Marni Lennon, Assistant Dean at the University of Miami School of Law.
- Accommodations requested and received and performance as a result, particularly if you can compare it favorably to previous academic performance.
- Accommodations on the LSAT were requested and were denied, and why this is a problem for you given the exact nature of your disability. If you have requested and received accommodations on any other standardized exam, include this information.

Does this strategy work? It can. If your GPA with accommodations is strong, and your SAT with accommodations was significantly higher (percentile wise) than your LSAT score, you can make a good argument.[14] If you have low grades and a low LSAT score (even with accommodations), you will need to make sure that other aspects of your application demonstrate that you have the skills necessary to be successful in law school. "Law schools should not be in the business of welcoming in students who they know, statistically, will not succeed in their programs; so, be thoughtful in your disclosures and how

---

[14] In the fall 2013 cycle, I had three clients for whom this was the case. Even though their GPAs were each at the 3.5 and up level, their LSAT scores were 141, 143, and 145 respectively. However, they all got into reach schools. But, temper your expectations; they are not attending top-25 law schools. However, they are getting into schools above the Florida Coastal/Thomas Cooley/Thomas Jefferson caliber, including Suffolk Law School and New York Law School.

you can provide strong examples of your success in particular courses, in the workplace, etc." said Marni Lennon, Assistant Dean of the University of Miami School of Law.

If you are deciding whether to share information about your disability with law schools, Lennon had the following comments:

> Some of your strategy may depend on how you fare on the LSAT and what your target schools are. If you end up in range for a law school without accommodations, you may consider whether disclosure is essential for your applications. Keep in mind that many schools benchmark against the LSAC and prior determinations when deciding what accommodations to provide in law school. The history of accommodations received in college, and before, will be evaluated as well, but it may be worth an anonymous phone call to your target school to gauge how determinations will be made.

CHAPTER 10

THE PERSONAL STATEMENT

What Is a Personal Statement?

THIS is the piece of your application over which, at present, you have the most control. And it's not to be taken lightly. A good personal statement adds to the application by tipping the scales in your favor. If someone with your numbers has a possibility of admission to a particular law school but not everyone with your numbers is admitted, the major deciding factor is the personal statement. A good letter of recommendation helps, but if you can't advocate for yourself, someone else advocating on your behalf isn't going to make your case for you. So, the personal statement is your chance to become more than a list of your accomplishments and experiences, more than your transcripts, and more than your LSAT score. This is your chance to be personable, likable, and impressive. This is your one chance to tell a law school what it wouldn't otherwise know about you. Don't blow it!

With that kind of pressure, it's understandable that this is the part of the application that makes you the most nervous. "I hate to write about myself!" you are saying to me. "I have no idea what to say!" you are thinking to yourself. "Nothing about me is unique!" you are screaming at your quasi-helpful parents. *What do I say to all of those fears? Get over them.*

What Do Law Schools Look for in a Personal Statement?

There are certain things a law school wants to be assured of: maturity despite youth, a commitment to the study of law, the ability to succeed in a rigorous environment, independent thinking skills, an understanding of the world around you, and feeling a duty greater than simple self-interest. Schools leave the topic pretty open to your choice.

New York University Law School says:

> Because people and their interests vary, we leave the content and length of your statement to your discretion. You may wish to complete or clarify your responses to items on the application form, bring to our attention additional information you feel should be considered, describe important or unusual aspects of yourself not otherwise apparent in your application, or tell us what led you to apply to NYU School of Law.[15]

Berkeley Law School describes it this way:

> There is no required topic for the statement. It is your opportunity to describe the subjective qualities that you will bring to the study of law at Berkeley. We recognize that there are many personal factors not measurable by one's academic record or test score,

---

[15] http://www.law.nyu.edu/admissions/jdadmissions/applicants/admissionsinformationan-dinstructions/index.htm

and that these factors are important to consider when building a law school class. Some of these factors include leadership potential, integrity and accountability, intellectual curiosity, determination in the face of adversity, problem-solving skills, resiliency, motivation, compassion, creativity, and the ability to relate well with people. Implicit in the value of a Berkeley Law degree is the caliber of our classroom dialogue. That dialogue is a function of the voices that comprise the class. Thus, your personal statement, first and foremost, should describe your voice. Because we do not interview applicants, the personal statement is your only opportunity to introduce yourself to us. Take advantage of this opportunity to describe your life journey, what brings you to our door, and perhaps why you wish to attend Berkeley Law School in particular.[16]

Arizona State's Sandra Day O'Connor College of Law says:

One of the goals of the Admissions Committee when making decisions is to admit a diverse student body that will contribute to a dynamic, interesting learning environment. Academic background and strength of performance, though important, are not the only criteria evaluated in the application process. For this reason, a personal statement, written by you, is required as part of the application. In this statement we seek information about you. Statements about law in general or law and society will not be useful. The statement should

---

[16] http://www.law.berkeley.edu/5188.htm

illustrate the life experiences and talents that make you unique. You are invited to write about significant obstacles that you have overcome and events in your life that influence your perspective.[17]

Elements of a Good Personal Statement

A good personal statement

- is interesting to read without needing to rely on shock value;
- has a conversational rather than formal tone;
- is not there to show how many big words you know;
- allows the law school to get to know you in a way it can't from other pieces of your application.

Will I Use the Same Essay for Every School?

Pretty much. A few schools ask for something a bit wacky (Colorado Law asks about leadership and character and the University of Florida[18] asks about academics).

California Western School of Law offers the option to send a personal statement on a topic of your choice or a 1- to 2-page essay on one of the following:

a. Write a personal statement about your expectations for what law school ought to be (e.g., focusing on issues such as what your expectations are, how do you know law school is right for you, what your life as a lawyer will be, or discuss a lawyer's role as a creative problem solver.

---

[17] http://www.law.asu.edu/admissions/Admissions/HowToApply.aspx

[18] http://www.law.ufl.edu/admissions/prospective-students/jd-application-procedures/the-jd-application

b. What is the most difficult thing you have ever had to do?

c. If you could relive any one day of your life, what day would it be?

d. At California Western, we make an effort to understand what you value, in order to provide support and guidance to your personal goals. Please attach a brief statement in which you discuss the personal values most important to you.

e. Write a statement on a topic of your choice.

On my blog you will find a list of all 200 law schools and a link to their personal statement requirements.[19] For most of them, the same personal statement will work. You will only tailor your essay to specific schools if (1) they ask you to do so; or (2) you have a very specific reason for wanting to attend and they do not ask for a "Why X Law School" optional essay.

How Long Should My Essay Be?

Some schools ask for only 500 words and others (Berkeley) allow for up to four pages double-spaced. However, most schools ask for a two-page (double-spaced) essay. Part of what you are being tested on is your ability to follow directions  (keeping to the length requirement) and the effectiveness of your writing. According to the Columbia Law website, "While there is no official page limit, a good guideline is two double-spaced pages, using readable fonts and margins. Your personal

---

[19] http://lawschoolexpert.com/personal-statements/
top-50-law-school-personal-statement-requirements/

statement/essay should be clear, concise, and an example of your best writing."[20]

Brevity rules. Almost every time I help edit a client's essay from three pages to two, the essay is improved by trimming the fat. I have yet to meet an essay that couldn't be cut and still be powerful. Cutting the length requires you to really think about your message and decide what is essential to include.

How Do I Decide on a Topic?

The biggest issue people face is choosing a topic. How do you attack this?

First, go negative. Make a list of your potential weaknesses as a law school applicant. This will help you decide what to show about yourself that is positive to counteract (indirectly!) any potential pitfalls. If you lack work experience and have never had to earn your own pocket money, you might appear to be a bit naive or self-centered. Do you need to compensate for lackluster grades by demonstrating intellectual ability and maturity?

Then, go positive. Many applicants stress themselves out trying to figure out what makes them unique. This is the wrong question to ask. Just think about who you are and what your best qualities and most meaningful experiences have been. Remove *uniqueness* from the equation and the pressure will be significantly relieved.

There is a misconception that personal statements must be about overcoming paralysis or poverty, or both. It's completely acceptable for someone who grew up with plenty of everything to want to attend law school and to deserve to get in. Just show some perspective. Show that you've done something

---

[20] http://web.law.columbia.edu/admissions/jd/apply/faq/application

meaningful with your life and that you've learned something relevant and insightful from your experiences (whatever they may have been).

The goal is to present a picture of you as someone who is ready for law school. You do not want to do this by directly addressing the question, but rather by telling a story that shows that you are a thinking person, someone who has experienced life, understands how the world works, and who brings something to the table that adds to a law school's class. You can do this by sharing a story about how your family background taught you the importance of working hard for what you want, how running a student organization taught you to deal with different situations, how your first career taught you what is most important as you embark on your second career, or how your chosen major(s) in college fueled your interest in law.

In recent years, due to the economy, law schools are particularly concerned with whether applicants have given serious thought to their future careers so that you do not turn out to be an unmotivated and/or disgruntled graduate of their law school. Therefore, some schools are asking you specifically to address motivations for studying law in their personal statement prompts. For example, here is the one from Boston College:

> We are interested particularly in learning about your motivation and preparation for the study of law as well as any circumstances that you believe relevant to the evaluation of your credentials.[21]

---

[21] http://www.bc.edu/content/bc/schools/law/admission/applying.html#procedure

When Should Something Be Your Personal Statement Topic as Opposed to Your Diversity Statement and/or Addendum?

If you are choosing a topic to explain circumstances surrounding poor grades in college, consider saving this story for your addendum and using your personal statement to address something positive. I had a client who originally was using a serious injury that was a setback during college as the subject for his personal statement, but instead I encouraged him to use that to explain a year of poor grades in college. This freed up his personal statement to address how a small town country boy went overseas and got his master's in international policy. Then he could write a diversity statement that piggy-backed on this by concentrating on the socio-economic background of his family and the poor level of educational resources in the town where he was raised. So, between these three documents, the reader got a really thorough glimpse into how three different aspects of his background overlapped and added to his perspective and experiences.

One of my clients wrote her personal statement about how being the child of immigrants motivated her to succeed in school, but found a different angle about this story (focusing on reliance on the kindness of others and the sacrifices made by her parents) for her diversity statement.

How Do I Brainstorm Topics?

When brainstorming topics, I find it can be helpful to sit down and write as much as possible in 30 minutes. Fill up as much space as you can for each topic and figure out which are easy to write about and which feel like a stretch.

When doing this exercise, try answering the following questions:

- What would surprise law schools (or even your best friends) to learn about you?
- What experiences in your life led you to law?
- What is your proudest accomplishment and why?
- What is the hardest thing you've ever done and what did you learn from it?
- Why did you choose a certain experience on your resume and how did it help you grow?
- How did your family life impact your decisions and experiences?
- What is a skill or attribute that defines you and what facts/stories from your background demonstrate that?

Examples

The following are some examples of different applicants and how to choose whether/how to present yourself given your backgrounds. They are not meant to be formulaic, but just examples of what you should think about when deciding how to present yourself to the law schools.

Professional Actor/Dancer/Musician

One of my clients wrote a compelling personal statement about how he developed from each of his majors (one in theatre and one in a pre-law subject). Another theatre major wrote about how he learned to work hard and do grunt work in summer stock, and how this has translated to his other endeavors. A professional dancer wrote about how she developed an eye for detail that applies to her professional endeavors today.

They were each very successful at getting into reach law schools even though they were initially worried that they would appear to be giving up on an artistic dream for a more pragmatic choice. You should also notice that none of them wrote about wanting to represent artists on becoming an attorney; that can be a bit unrealistic and cliché. It is important to show how law school fits into their goals, but it doesn't have to be so predictable as picking an area of law to practice. If it does so naturally, fine, but you do not need to force it for your story to make sense.

Teach for America

Want to influence public policy on education now that you've been in the classroom and seen the impact of education inequity? I believe you, and I believe in what you are trying to do, I promise; however, it's been said by every Teach for America (TFA) participant who has ever applied to law school. TFA is a highly regarded program, with great training, and they pick the best and brightest. It's a credibility builder with law schools, and social justice is something law schools care about so you are already ahead. But if you're going to write about this in your personal statement, try to take a different approach with it (special education advocacy or speaking a foreign language), or highlight something else about your background and leave TFA to a letter of recommendation and to your resume. One thing— if you are a TFA person PLEASE, PLEASE, PLEASE, don't tell me the story of poor little Micah or Isabelle who comes from a family living at the poverty level and how he or she is facing every disadvantage and how by working with his or her family you learned X and Y. This is not your story. When Micah or Isabelle applies to law school in fifteen years, I look forward to reading their essays about how a teacher inspired them to reach higher and help others. But their story is not your story.

Your personal statement needs to tell something personal about you. It can't focus more on someone else just because you led a privileged life. Otherwise it comes off as, "I met someone who was poor at least…."

Study Abroad

Studying abroad is so common now, that for about five years I've had a rule with my clients—no essays about studying abroad. For a while, it was cute to read stories about how the lights turned on automatically in the stairwells in Italy and how you learned to drive on the left in London or Melbourne, but now these things have lost their luster because they end up sounding naive.

The Scattered Soul

Have you dabbled in a lot of things but not become the master of any? Emphasize that you take initiative in the things you do and that you learn from each opportunity. Demonstrate that you are not just a person skating through another boring summer; show that you really put effort into understanding the field. One of my clients maintained a crafts blog and another monitored an online gaming community; both are now graduates of Top-14 law schools. Don't underestimate what you have going for you even if it feels unrelated to law school.

Internships

You should choose to emphasize your internships in a personal statement *only* if you learned something specific in a unique situation, were able to contribute meaningfully, or learned something significant from having a negative experience at an internship. Think about what makes the experience interesting. Simply having the internship on your resume and explaining your duties may be enough to "get credit" for it, opening up your personal statement for something more insightful about your character and experiences. But, if you can show initiative, that you are self-motivated, that you give yourself the freedom to make mistakes and learn from them, that you exercise good judgment and independent thought, this will go a long way toward presenting your internship experiences effectively in a personal statement.

Case Study Example:

> One of my clients had a very strong GPA from a very good undergraduate school, and an LSAT score just below the 25th percentile of most of the Top 10 schools. Her resume was packed with everything pre-law, including a thesis on a constitutional issue. Her personal statement, rather than being a cheerleading piece for her resume, was about learning that she was not meant for political work after spending a summer working on Capitol Hill. She is now attending Yale Law School.

Significant Experience in Real Estate, Finance, Computer Science, Etc.

If you worked on projects that interfaced with law, this can help you provide a good tie-in to a natural move to law school. If you were self-employed, you can repackage your experience as knowing how to run a business. You can use your work experience to show problem-solving skills, people skills, and other experiences that will prove helpful as a lawyer in private practice.

Demonstrate that you know what you are getting yourself into with the financial and time investment of returning to school.

Paralegal (More Than 2 Years)

One thing you really have going for you is a clear understanding of what lawyers do and what it takes to be a successful attorney. You know the kind of attorney you want to be, and the kind of attorney you pray you'll never become. Use this to your advantage! You could write about the longest day you had, the hardest thing you did on the job, what this experience taught you about your future career (good and bad), a particular case that moved you or frustrated you. Tons to work with here!

What Should I Avoid?

Generally, I urge people to stay away from an essay that revolves around high school. You can use childhood experiences to provide context for later decisions/events that you will be discussing, but they shouldn't be more than half of your essay. If you suffered a traumatic event as a child that created the necessity for you to work full-time while in school or remain close to home, there is a good reason to share that event because it provides context to your later achievements and decisions. High school sports should never be mentioned. *Ever.* Neither should high school mock trial competitions. These are the things that got you into college. What have you done since then to get yourself into law school? What you did as a teenager while under your parents' roof is not going to impress anyone, unless you are the person who is applying to law school at age 18.

Here are examples of topics to avoid:

- The injured athlete who struggled to find his way after no longer having the structure and support system of the team.
- Study abroad, particularly of the "learning to drive on the other side of the road" variety.
- Writing about an event that the entire country experienced as being your impetus for applying to law school unless you were intimately involved or directly impacted.
- Sharing a story that really makes you a high-maintenance complainer, such as the time you fought the dean of your school over your B+.
- A childhood dream of becoming a lawyer, particularly one that includes a cute story about how you negotiated your bedtime or decided to become a lawyer after watching a certain TV legal drama.

Here are things to watch out for:

As director of admissions for law schools, I would groan, roll my eyes, and write sarcastic comments on personal statements hinting of the following:

- Arrogance and elitism.
- A purported drive to serve others and to "be a voice for the voiceless," particularly where this is not supported by anything you've actually done in the past.
- Talking about someone else's challenges and how they inspired you.
- Repeating a resume.
- Providing lots of conclusions with few facts to back

them up. A good personal statement never has to say, "I always wanted to be a lawyer," or "I overcame obstacles" or "I work hard" because the story being told convinces the reader to come to this conclusion on his or her own.

- Not being specific and talking around issues instead of addressing them directly.
- Spelling and punctuation errors.
- Excessive use of passive voice.
- Being "too" memorable. Some applicants believe the goal is to be so memorable that they will be remembered, but this really only happens when an essay is so ridiculous that it becomes a joke in the admissions office or when an applicant's life story is so compelling that it's not an essay you could even try to write if it weren't absolutely and completely authentic.
- Treatises on the importance of law in society.
- Quotes by famous people, not said directly (and only) to you.
- Being artsy/poetic.
- Failure to follow directions or answer the question being asked.
- Including the school's name as a fill-in-the-blank without saying anything meaningful about the school.
- Using any of the following words or phrases:

  o Personally—It's a personal statement. By you. Of course it's personal.
  o In Conclusion—Blech. Just conclude. Don't announce that you're concluding.
  o I believe—It really doesn't matter what you believe

about your ability to succeed in law school. The fact that you believe it is immaterial. Just state the facts so that the reader independently concludes that he or she believes what you are trying to prove. (Same with "I think").

o   Unique —Very few things in this world are unique, especially the use of the word "unique."

o   Firsthand—I think it goes without saying that your experiences are firsthand. What else would they be? And if they were second-hand, why would you write about them?

What Should My Introduction Look Like?

I want to learn one relevant fact about you from the introduction of your essay. I do not care if you have a "hook" or clever attention-getting device. I would prefer something straightforward and professional that gets me interested in you right from the beginning. I do not want you to introduce your story with vague statements like "My life has been a journey" or "I am the culmination of my experiences." These are lame statements, not only because they can be heard on any episode of *The Bachelor,* but because they apply to everybody. I learn nothing about you. Instead, start with a fact.

Here are a few examples with some explanations of what the applicants were trying to accomplish:

Area of Specialization

> *"I sat in a lecture hall at New York University School of Law, completely surrounded by men with some—or less—hair. Timidly, I glanced at my fellow attendees. Would they accept me as a member? I tried to listen to*

the conversations happening around me, and find a time to join in, but it seemed like everyone had known each other for years. I had just joined the Copyright Society of America."

This client had a great LSAT score and poor grades, and her resume was heavy on artistic endeavors. By writing about her involvement in the Copyright Society, she demonstrated a clear reason for attending law school and showed she had the chutzpah to take the initiative to accomplish her goals. She got into Fordham Law School off the waiting list, is now a graduate of Fordham Law School and serves as general counsel for a corporation in New York.

Young Applicant

"I spent only three short years in college, but I used them to the fullest, often taking sixteen to twenty credits a semester in order to explore subjects not required for my major. My education was enhanced because, once I began with a subject, I continued to explore it in as many ways as I could."

This client attended a great college but only had two years' of transcripts by the time she submitted her application. We wanted to show that there was more to her transcripts that met the eye: yes, her grades were very good, and she had internships with a large corporation, but she was also more than just those things, and this essay went on to describe her interest in religions, the environment, math, sciences and law, and how her interdisciplinary studies helped her growth and direction for her career. She was admitted to several Top-14 schools.

INTERNATIONAL Student/Music Major

> *"I came to America by myself when I was seventeen.*
> *I wanted to attend college in the United States, but*
> *without knowing a word of English, it seemed like a*
> *distant dream. I chose to attend a boarding school in*
> *order to immerse myself in an English-speaking envi-*
> *ronment. My dedication to academic success in a new*
> *language took many forms, including studying in the rest-*
> *room every night after lights-out in the dorm."*

This essay focused on dedication to goals by showing how the writer was willing to put in long hours to reach his goals. It brought his story forward to show how he taught music lessons during college (mostly in exchange for free food); even as he transitioned out of music as a professional, he kept the same dedication and applied it to all of his other endeavors.

Troubled Start to College with Complete Turnaround

> *"I have been a recovering alcoholic since June 14,*
> *2007. While addiction is a life-long struggle, with the*
> *support of family, friends, and my intense desire to make*
> *something of my life, I have demonstrated through my*
> *commitment to education and to service that I am pre-*
> *pared for the demands of the legal profession."*

This client took a leave of absence from college to participate in rehabilitation, and then returned to a non-traditional college program. He excelled and was granted acceptance to the regular degree program, where he continued to excel. His essay talked about this, and how he went on to mentor troubled youth. With a very high GPA and a low 150s LSAT score, he was admitted to several reach schools. He chose to attend a Top 100 school, where he is in the top 5 percent of his class.

Professional Poker Player

> *"A computer programmer, a physicist, an immigrant from Vietnam who never graduated from high school, a taxi driver, and a young man wearing a backward baseball cap are all sitting around a table with me. We are chatting and laughing. In most circumstances, we appear to be an unlikely group. However, the wide variety of people I meet and interact with is one of the things about poker that I find most interesting."*

This client had an undergraduate degree from Berkeley with unimpressive grades, and more than a few years of floundering before deciding to apply to law school. Her personal statement showed thoughtfulness and sophistication, and shared a very different side of poker with the reader and shattered stereotypes: she shared how poker players banded together to raise money for someone among their ranks who became ill. She is a graduate of the University of California at Irvine College of Law.

Growing Up on a Farm

> *"My parents did not want us to associate work with monetary gain alone, but rather with life itself. For me, hard work is as regular as waking up in the morning, and when you grow up on a ranch with five siblings, that means getting up at 5 a.m.; any later and you risk an additional two hours of shoveling horse manure."*

This client went on to discuss how her family was able to adapt when the recession hit, and how working hard with a positive attitude paid off when she worked selling cars and when she faced a serious health issue. This client had a low 140s LSAT score but a 3.5 GPA, and her essay about hard work led to her admission to several law schools where the median LSAT score is fifteen points higher than hers.

Parents as Attorneys

> "Despite their common profession as attorneys, my protective Chinese mother and jolly, comforting Caucasian father raised me from very different perspectives."

This client had a 3.9 and a mid-160s LSAT score. His essay went on to talk about how different his parents' careers were, and how each one influenced his desire to be a lawyer. However, we did not want it to seem like attending law school was a default decision for him so we made it clear that he seriously considered whether the career was right for him. He has been admitted to several Top-14 law schools.

Student Leadership

> "Being thrown into the fire of my fraternity's executive board as a freshman helped me develop as a leader."

This client spent a lot of time as a leader of his fraternity, but we used examples from his leadership experiences that showed the business and people skills he developed as treasurer and then president of his fraternity, and how he worked to bring the organization to a better place.

Diversity Topic as Personal Statement

> *"Bombay Riots, India, 1992: It was all very real to me. The Hindu Muslim riots that shook the country, and the world, were happening on the streets outside my house. I have a vivid memory of seeing my father bring his guns out, layer our terrace with broken glass, and keep watch throughout the night. This is my first memory associated with religion."*

This applicant could have written one student leadership essay and one diversity statement, but since her diversity statement was not about an obstacle overcome but rather a cultural experience growing up in India that led her to get involved in religious freedom-related issues in college, it worked beautifully as a personal statement.

Second Career

> *"Years ago, I thought that I would have to wait until I became a successful professional in order to do anything meaningful with my life. When my original career plans in veterinary medicine unexpectedly changed, however, I realized that I can make a difference by simply using the resources that I already have at my disposal."*

This applicant was in her 40s. She had to leave graduate school more than twenty years prior because of family responsibilities. In her essay, she wrote about how she strived to help others' lives as much as she could without a law degree but that this was finally the time to pursue law as a means of serving others.

Personally Insightful

> *"I spotted two young couples on a blanket, doing their best to look away from me as they shouted, "Look! It's a beached whale!" The situation was all too familiar. It remains acceptable to criticize and discriminate against fat people. I knew exactly what was going on: these strangers were throwing me verbal harpoons."*

This client had great credentials, including a master's in library science, and looked great on paper, but I wanted her to show that she was also an insightful and feeling person. Her essay went on to discuss how she could relate to people who were marginalized by society and her sensitivity to stereotypes, but the best part was her conclusion, where she shared that she actually approached the couples who had so cruelly insulted her, intending to embarrass them, but she ended up talking with them, joining them on their blanket, and how one of them opened up to her about how he used to be overweight and had felt very badly joining in the joke.

This client recently graduated from Northwestern Law and is a federal public defender.

How Do I Conclude My Personal Statement?

Personal statements conclude somewhat formulaically, which is better than a cute ending, trust me. Lawyers make their arguments, conclude clearly (not cleverly), and get out. Your personal statement should be the same. The body should make your case, and the end doesn't need to repeat, echo a cute opening, or bring anything full circle. It should end with something about law school. *Pretty much every time. Pretty much without exception.*

- How did the experience you shared lead you to law school?
- How did it help you develop qualities that prepared you for law school?
- How did it help you develop interests that you hope to explore in law school and/or at a particular law school?

Addressing one or more of these issues (depending on your personal statement topic) is the way to conclude an effective and persuasive personal statement.

How Do I Format My Essay?

Standard rule is to use a serif-font (with little lines on the end of letters), in 12-point, double-spaced, with 1 inch margins all around. Use a header that has your name, LSAC ID#, and the title, "Personal Statement," and page number on each page of every document you upload with an application. *Do not use a title other than Personal Statement. Ever.* I see people try things like, "A Journey to Law" or even something they perceive as clever, and it never works.

CHAPTER 11

WRITING OPTIONAL ESSAYS

Should You Submit an "Optional" Essay?

MANY law schools provide opportunities to submit a second essay (and even a third) with their applications. Sometimes it's a "Diversity Statement," and sometimes it's referred to as an optional essay and a particular topic is provided. Some of these topics are addressed below as examples.

If an optional essay applies to your situation and does not repeat your personal statement, then you really should do the essay, even if a school says that your admission chances won't be impacted should you choose not to do it. Not only does the essay provide you with another opportunity to show something new about yourself, but it's also a way to show you really are interested in the school because you went the extra mile in your application to create something just for them.

Here are Typical Topics for Optional Essays:

Diversity

Be careful here because there are two kinds of diversity statements.

One asks about obstacles overcome.

The other asks about how you will add to the diversity of the law school.[22]

These are very different questions. Why? Because lots of people add diversity and few people have had their diversity factors serve as obstacles to overcome. If you are the child of immigrants who came to this country penniless and shared a one-bedroom apartment with six family members while you were growing up, and your non-English speaking parents washed dishes at a restaurant as their second jobs at night, then you probably are familiar with obstacles and with overcoming them. If you are from a culturally diverse background but grew up with every (or nearly every) privilege, you can probably write a good essay about learning from two different cultures, but only the second essay prompt applies to you. See the difference?

Everyone has a gay best friend or a friend who is Muslim: please don't write about someone else's struggle and try to get points for empathizing or appreciating the struggles of others.

---

[22] For example, "In addition to your personal statement, you may wish to provide an additional essay. This essay is your opportunity to discuss any aspect of your background or life experience that you believe will enhance your ability to contribute to the diverse BU [Boston University] classroom experience and community. BU Law values and recognizes the importance of diversity. An ethnically, socio-economically and otherwise diverse class is essential to the education of each student. As a producer of leaders in legal practice, government or other public service, academia and business, BU Law continues its long-standing tradition of providing opportunities for persons of all backgrounds and providing the excellent training to which a diverse classroom is indispensable."http://www.bu.edu/law/prospective/apply/jd/application/#howh

This is *your* law school application, and it has to be about you. If you wrote about your struggles as a minority or as a single mother in your personal statement, don't repeat those things here. You could, potentially, use your personal statement as your diversity statement and write your personal statement on something entirely different for schools that have the option of both. If you have overcome significant obstacles in your life, there are some law schools with programs such as Legal Education Opportunity Program (LEOP) that have separate applications and admission criterion. One example of this is University of California, Hastings College of Law.[23]

Why X Law School

This question has been increasingly popular on law school applications: the University of Pennsylvania, University of Michigan, Tulane Law School, UC Irvine, and Loyola Chicago are among the schools that ask for an "optional" essay about your interest in their school. Why is it important that you are interested in the school? Because of *yield protection*. What is this? Schools are ranked, largely, upon their admission criteria and their acceptance rates. As a result, law schools are very protective of these numbers. Therefore, they don't want to hand out acceptances to people they feel are unlikely to attend. This is why people with very strong numbers are often waitlisted at schools (read: Georgetown Law). We will discuss this further in Chapter 16, "Waitlists, Deferrals, Holds, and Reserve Lists."

So, if a school asks you why you are interested, you need to show you've done some research. Most school websites are pretty thorough, especially if you look beyond the "Prospective

[23] http://www.uchastings.edu/admissions/jd/how-apply/index.php

Student" pages and really explore the activities of the faculty and students.

Here are some things to mention:

- Any specific ties you have to the school (friends who are at the law school, parents who attended, a supervisor who is a graduate) or to the area (your parents moved there recently, etc.);

- The similarities (collegial atmosphere, college town versus urban atmosphere, etc.) between that campus and your college campus (assuming you've been successful in that environment in the past);

- A particular focus of the law school (that you are sure is real and active and substantial) that matches with a specific interest that is evident from your activities such as an environmental or immigration law clinic that matches with volunteer efforts you've done in the past.

- That you have met with someone at the law school or visited the school, and the law school in particular, and any observations or things you learned that impressed you.

- If you are applying for the part-time program (usually for NON-TRADITIONAL applicants), explain why this is the good fit for you so that they do not think you are applying to that program because of a perception that it is easier to get in. (See Chapter 14, "Choosing a Law School," for a discussion on whether to apply to a part-time program.)

Things to avoid:

- Claiming that a school's environmental law program is the reason you are applying when there is nothing in your background to show any connection to environmental issues.
- Mentioning a summer study abroad program as your reason for applying because you can (generally) participate in any law school's study abroad program no matter where you attend.
- Overly broad statements that could be applied to almost any law school (what I call "brochure text") such as "esteemed faculty" or "renowned faculty" or "national reputation" or "impressive bar passage rate." Be more specific.
- Usually, Harvard, Yale, Stanford, and Columbia aren't so concerned with yield. They know you'll pretty much enroll if you're admitted. So you don't need to say "Why Harvard." Duh. It's Harvard.

Thoughtful Essays

The University of Pennsylvania and University of Michigan Law have optional essay topics that are fairly serious. For example, in the past, the University of Pennsylvania has offered the opportunity for applicants to respond to one or more of the following topics:

- Describe how your background or experiences will enhance the diversity of the Penn Law community (e.g., based on your culture, race, ethnicity, religion, sexual orientation, ideology, age, socioeconomic status, academic background, employment, or personal experience).

- Dean Michael A. Fitts has highlighted the core strengths that make Penn Law the best place to receive a rigorous and engaging legal education: genuine integration with associated disciplines; transformative, forward-looking faculty scholarship; highly-regarded experiential learning through urban clinics and our pro bono pledge; innovative, hands-on global engagement; and a manifest commitment to professional development and collegiality. These are the qualities that define Penn Law. What defines you? How do your goals and values match Penn Law's core strengths?

- Describe a time when, as a member of a team, you particularly excelled or were especially frustrated. What was your role within that team? What was the outcome?

- If you do not think that your academic record or standardized test scores accurately reflect your ability to succeed in law school, please tell us why.

The last one is the easiest since it's basically the addendum you've already drafted for other schools to cover these topics. So don't just do that one and pat yourself on the back for doing optional essays. The first one is the diversity statement, but trimmed to one page. The second is one that should be impossible to ignore: if you're trying to make the case that Penn is the right place for you, you should be able to answer this question. The team member one has the potential to be done very well—I've seen good essays on this written by musicians as part of groups and by applicants who worked in groups in an MBA program. It's pretty open-ended and gives you the chance to highlight a professional experience in a new way. (The "team" essay is not the time to talk about your high school football glory days.)

The Silly Essays

I love that Georgetown Law doesn't take itself too seriously. Here are the five optional essay topics they used for the Fall 2013 admission cycle:

1. Tell us about a time when you failed and what you learned.
2. What is the best advice you ever received and have you followed it?
3. Describe your perfect day. Ever have one?
4. How would your friends describe you? Did they miss anything?
5. Prepare a one-minute video that says something about you.

These questions suck if you take them too seriously. But if you try to get creative, these can actually be fun to attack. Of course, each essay is limited to 250 words, but think of that as a relief. It's only two paragraphs! I've read some fabulous answers to #1, #2, and #4 but the answer to #3 is really hard to do without talking about sunsets and great breakfasts and being with family and friends, blah, blah, blah. If you pick #1, pick something that's a real failure, not a "fake failure" like the time you only got a B+ on a test but worked really hard to come back to earn an "A" in the class.

I've seen some great videos by those who dare. With planning and editing, you can say quite a lot in 60 seconds and it definitely lets the reader get to know you a bit more as a person. But show the video around to people before you submit it: make sure you don't speak too quickly, seem cocky, fake, or odd in some unexpected way.

The 250-Word Open-Ended Essay

Yale is famous for this one. My clients who have been admitted to Yale all used this essay to share something about themselves that would not have been evident elsewhere in the application.[24] On shorter essays, really think about each word you choose to use. Avoid repetition. Get right to your point. Most importantly, know what your point is.

---

[24] Yale Law School's blog has great tips for do's and don'ts for this essay. http://blogs.law.yale.edu/blogs/admissions/archive/2008/01/23/the-250-word-albatross.aspx

CHAPTER 12

THE APPLICATION TIMELINE

When Should You Apply to Law School?

L AW school applications become available between the end of August and the beginning of October. Most schools state deadlines somewhere between February 1 and June 1. However, 99 percent of law schools start admitting people shortly after applications become available (in October and November). It is important to note that many schools use *rolling admissions*—beginning to accept students as soon as the admissions period begins. If you wait to apply in time for the deadlines (in the spring), schools (all of them but Yale) have already admitted enough people to fill their classes and already have people on waiting lists. As a result, unless your application is really stellar, with high numbers for that school, it's hard to be competitive for admission late in the application cycle.

Should You Apply Before Having Your LSAT Score?

Usually, no. Your application will not be reviewed until it is "complete," and it can't be complete without an LSAT score. Besides, until the score comes in, you don't know if you'll even be competitive at a school. You may also miss the opportunity to explain an LSAT score as part of your application if you later decide an explanation would be prudent.

Remember that it takes 3 to 4 weeks after you take the LSAT to get your score. Once you have your score, you may decide to apply to different schools and/or to re-take the LSAT.

Is There an Advantage to Applying on the Very First Day?

No. Absolutely not. Law school admission officers spend most of August through November at recruiting events (giving out precious fee waivers and trying to drum up interest in their schools). It's hard to spend much time in September reviewing files. Trust me, when I was on the bus with all of the other admission officers, bouncing from Marriott to Marriott, standing behind tables answering questions from potential applicants for hours at a time, lugging heavy brochures, I was not reading files during my free time.

Besides, it's a better idea to take a few extra weeks to submit the highest quality product, the best possible personal statement and resume, rather than a rushed one. Early Decision and Early Notification deadlines are usually between November 1 and November 15 (with some schools holding out until December or March to give you a chance to be denied from your real first choice law school); so certainly, any applications submitted before Thanksgiving are pretty early.

If you are sticking with a June LSAT score, submit your applications in September/October. If you are working with an October LSAT score, submit applications in November/December. You can absolutely make Early Decision and Early Notification deadlines with a September/October LSAT score if you plan ahead. If you are taking the December LSAT, plan to submit applications by mid-January. I still believe the February LSAT is too late to be really competitive for admission the same fall. However, if you really rock the LSAT, then mid-range schools will find a place for you. Be realistic, however, reach schools will be even more of a reach at this time of year.

What Is the Latest Date to Apply and Still Take Advantage of Rolling Admissions?

When I wrote the first edition of this book in 2009, law school application numbers were at an all-time high, and I stressed the importance of applying by December to be competitive. For the 2013 cycle, however, I had more clients still applying in January and February, and that was perfectly acceptable considering that (at that time) applications to law school had decreased 38 percent over the previous two years.

Remember that anyone taking the December LSAT is probably spending the winter holidays on application materials. It can be stressful to find time to work on applications with family demands, and, of course, it's usually storm and flu season, which can hamper things. Plan ahead and don't save everything for winter break. There are schools that ask you to apply before a date in January to be competitive for certain scholarships, so keep your eye on those deadlines, too.[25]

If you decide to take the February LSAT the same year that you hope to start law school, take some time to consider an alternative strategy. If you are graduating from college, it might be good to take a year off and let schools see your senior year grades and to gain some work/travel/volunteer experience while giving yourself more time to put applications together and study for the LSAT. NON-TRADITIONAL applicants often

---

[25] www.law.nyu.edu/admissions/jdadmissions/applicants/applications/index.htm

worry about getting another year older and delaying law school; they often feel rushed to apply and go wherever they can get in. But this is often a poor decision in the long term, especially where insufficient time has been spent preparing for the LSAT and perfecting application materials. Besides, taking a year to save some money for law school would be a sound long-term decision. If you've been laid off recently and you need to be in school for the loans, please really reconsider. Law school is a huge investment; *you need to be invested in the process* and take the time to make sure that this is really a sound financial/career direction for you.[26] I am a big believer in making the smarter long-term decision over the convenient short-term decision. After all, usually the people who applied at the last minute and chose to attend whatever law school would take them are the ones who try to transfer the following year; however, unless you have grades at the top of your 1L class, it's very hard to transfer. (See Chapter 19, "Transferring Law Schools.")

I have a great infographic on the law school admission timeline on my website. Be sure to check it out:

http://lawschoolexpert.com/uncategorized/
the-time-is-now-to-get-into-law-school-infographic/.

What Is an Early Decision Program?

One of the first decisions you'll have to make after solidifying your schools list is whether to apply under an Early Decision program. These programs usually have early deadlines and require you to state that you will absolutely and unequivocally attend if you are granted admission by a certain date. Most schools are pretty straightforward: Apply by November 1st or November 15th and get a decision in December. If you

---

[26] For more on whether law school is the right decision for you, take time to read The Law School Decision Game.

are accepted, you withdraw all other applications and send your deposit.

The rule with Early Decision applications is that this is a binding agreement you are making with the school; if admitted, you will attend that school and withdraw all applications from other schools. In return, you will receive your admission decision a little bit faster (usually before Winter Break). The caveat is that in many cases your application will simply be deferred until the regular admissions cycle. But Early Decision is a great option for that school that you know, no matter what, you would attend. (See the explanation offered at Duke Law School's website.[27])

---

[27] The following is from Duke Law's website: "The program is most appropriate for candidates who have concluded that Duke is their first-choice for law school. Applicants who are admitted through our early decision program are reviewed for scholarship assistance on the same basis as all other admitted students, although they do not have the opportunity to compare offers from other schools. In recognition of their high level of interest in Duke, all admitted Early Decision applicants who apply for need-based scholarship consideration will receive a $15,000 Early Decision Grant, in addition to any additional award for which they are eligible. Candidates who apply through the Early Decision program may apply to other law schools, but may not have more than one binding Early Decision application pending simultaneously. If an Early Decision application has already been submitted to another law school, candidates may apply through Duke's Early Decision program only if and when they are released from their binding commitment at the other school. If admitted to Duke Law School, Early Decision candidates will be required to immediately withdraw their applications at other law schools, refrain from submitting new applications, and submit a $500 tuition deposit no later than ten days after the admission notification. Round I Early Decision candidates must submit the application no later than November 12, 2012. Applications must be complete no later than December 3, 2012. Duke Law School will notify Round I Early Decision candidates about their status no later than December 31, 2012. Round II Early Decision candidates must submit the application no later than January 7, 2013 and be complete no later than January 18, 2013. Duke Law School will notify Round II Early Decision candidates about their status no later than January 31, 2013. Some Early Decision candidates may be held for review in the regular cycle; candidates who are held for consideration in the regular cycle will no longer be bound by the terms of the Early Decision agreement. Duke Law School reserves the right to provide other law schools with the names of candidates admitted through the binding Early Decision program."

Georgetown Law's program has a deadline that isn't until March, but flat-out warns you that if financial aid is part of your decision-making process, you shouldn't apply under their Early Decision program.[28] At least Duke and George Washington are among the schools that offer scholarships to applicants admitted under the binding program: that way you don't have to worry that you'll be losing out on scholarship offers to other schools by applying under the binding program.

If a scholarship to another school would lure you away, or if a girlfriend/boyfriend moving to another city would change your desire to attend that school, please do not apply Early Decision. Many people ask me about "gaming" the system— will they get into a huge reach school because they have bound themselves to attend? The answer really is "no." Early Decision works best for the person with a 3.8 GPA and 169 LSAT who applies Early Decision at Columbia Law and wants to stay in New York for personal reasons, or for the person who doesn't think he or she'll be competitive at UC Irvine and has to stay in Orange County and, therefore, applies Early Decision at Chapman Law.

Early Decision Deadlines are absolutely available for October LSAT takers; just have everything in your application ready to go when you get your LSAT score because some schools have Early Decision deadlines on November 1; Most are November 15, and some are even on a rolling basis. (See New York University Law's website.)

University of Pennsylvania has two rounds of binding early decision. One is for people who apply by November 15th (with an LSAT score from October or before) with applicants receiving a decision by the end of December. December LSAT takers (and applicants who have already been rejected from their real first-choice law schools) may apply under a Round 2 of the Early Decision program in January. Duke also has a second round in January. University of Virginia has a lenient date of applying under their program and says they will make a decision within 15 days of your file being complete. (One of my clients this year got her acceptance letter under this program within three days of applying.) This kind of certainty is an extreme relief to many law school applicants.

What Does the Law School Do with My Application When It Receives It?

The first thing a law school does when it receives your application is check to make sure it is complete. Are the questions answered properly? Did you attach the correct documents? Did you leave any questions blank? Then the school waits for your LSAC Credential Assembly Service Report, including your LSAT score(s), transcripts, Academic Summary Report, and the letters of recommendation you have designated for that school. CAS forwards these items as they receive them, so even if you haven't taken the LSAT yet they will go ahead and send the other items. However, the law school won't do a single thing with your file until it has absolutely all of these items.

Once your application is deemed "complete," it will be put into one of three piles. At many schools, these piles are based on index numbers. The index calculation is based on your LSAT (the highest at most schools but the average at a few schools) and UGPA. Based simply on the numbers, your file will be presumed to be either a *presumptive admit*, *presumptive deny*, or *committee file* (somewhere in the middle).

At most schools, the director of admissions is making most

decisions single-handedly. One Dean of Admissions told me that it's common for only 10 percent of files to be forwarded to the faculty committee. This was certainly my experience as director of admissions for two law schools.

If your numbers make you a presumptive admit, then your file will most likely be reviewed by someone in the admission office. If everything is strong and there are no red flags, signs of weirdness or arrogance, or character and fitness violations, you'll probably be admitted right off the bat. Easy! If there are some concerns, your file will be passed along to the committee (see below).

If your numbers place you in the presumptive deny pile, then someone in the admission office will read through your application for soft factors, explanations, review of your essay(s), resume, letters of recommendation, etc. If something in there catches their eye, you will be bumped up for committee review. This happens all the time. However, if your numbers are low and there are problems with your application and/or candidacy beyond the numbers, you will no longer be in the running. Watch the online status checker for "decision mailed."[29]

If you are in the middle pile, then someone in the admission office takes some notes and passes the file along to members of the faculty admission committee for their review, comments, and votes. This takes a while because faculty members on the whole are not a speedy bunch. They have classes and vacations and those pesky office hours and faculty meetings. But this is where your file gets ranked as someone who will be admitted, waitlisted, held for a later decision, or rejected.

This process explains why two people whose applications

---

[29] I'm kidding. This isn't always what this means.

are complete on the same day may receive decisions months apart from each other.

Once you are admitted, your file is reviewed for scholarship consideration. (See Chapter 18, "Scholarships" for more information.)

When Should You Expect to Hear Back?

Some schools are awesome about getting back to you quickly (Duke Law's 10-day priority application and the University of Miami come to mind), but others will keep you waiting even past the April deadline that they give themselves for getting back to applicants. If your file is "clean" (without any "red flags" or issues that require further consideration) and your numbers are solid for a school (at or above the medians), then you will probably hear back fairly quickly. If you responded affirmatively[30] to character and fitness questions (see Chapter 9, "Explaining Your Weaknesses"), then your application will take longer because more people will have to sign off on it before a decision is made. Of course, some schools don't review applications for a while, and they send out result letters in batches, usually because they are understaffed.

---

[30] Saying "Yes" or checking the box that you had these items to report.

CHAPTER 13

FILLING OUT APPLICATIONS

What Do I Need to Decide Before Filling Out Applications?

- Will you be applying under an Early Decision program? (Go back to Chapter 12, "The Application Timeline" for more information.)
- Will you be applying full time or part time?

Here are some things to consider:

- If you have not been in school for a long time, haven't been the world's best student, and/or you would like to continue working during your first year of law school, then consider applying part time to law schools that offer this as an option. You will take one less class each semester, and if you make up the two classes during the summer after your first year, you can usually transfer into the full time program and graduate in three years. Otherwise, you are not permitted to work during your first year of law school. It is permitted to work up to 20 hours per week as a

2L and 3L, or full time if you attend law school only
part time.[31]

- It is not possible to "dabble" in law school. You will
  not be able to take one or two classes at a time until
  you finally graduate. The American Bar Association
  (ABA) requires that you finish your degree no later
  than 84 months after starting law school.[32] This can't
  be re-set by transferring schools.

- If you begin law school part time and then want to
  transfer to another law school, you will most likely be
  restricted to transferring to another part-time program
  because you will not have earned a sufficient number
  of credits to be compared with other 1Ls and/or to
  begin your second year of law school.

- Do you want to have a social life? If you would be
  happiest surrounded by students who may be older,
  working, married, with families and/or with professional careers under their belts, then you would
  probably be very comfortable in a part-time program.
  If, however, you will deeply regret the sounds of joy
  coming from the Quad during Thursday night keg
  parties sponsored by the Student Bar Association
  while you are stuck in Contracts or Torts, then
  attending school at night probably isn't a good idea.

- Some law schools offer year-round two-year J.D.
  programs. One of my former clients who was ten

---

[31] There are ABA rules regulating these things, and if you are curious about work restrictions and related issues, you should look into these rules. www.americanbar.org/content/
dam/aba/migrated/legaled/standards/20072008standardsWebContent/Chapter_3.auth-
checkdam.pdf

[32] ABA Standard 304 (c)

years out of college decided to do Southwestern Law School's SCALE program and saved $40,000.

- If you are an INTERNATIONAL student, you are not going to be able to attend law school part time under your visa restrictions.

What Should I Know Before Filling Out Applications?

First, the process is all online through LSAC. Thank God. What you enter for one application is (mostly) automatically completed in subsequent applications. But there are still a lot of opportunities for mistakes.

Here are things to keep in mind:

- Make sure to fill out every question that is required.
- Make sure your responses fit in the space provided. Sometimes things are cut off rather awkwardly.
- Check punctuation and capitalization.
- Do not check too many areas of interest of law, and don't say you are interested in something just because you think a school is known for it. Make sure your stated area(s) of interest are consistent with other areas of your application.
- Attach the correct documents.
- Don't attach anything extra with your application such as copies of your thesis or newspaper articles.
- Be sure that tracked changes aren't showing up on your attached documents because LSAC turns your Word documents into PDFs when you attach them.
- Check each school's website and application instructions to be sure you are submitting exactly what the law school is looking for.

- Make sure employment dates are consistent between your application and your resume.
- Make sure your formatting is consistent between all attachments: usually this means double spacing with a serif-font (e.g., Times New Roman), 11 or 12 point in size, with one-inch margins and a header on each page that includes your name, LSAC ID#, the document heading (Personal Statement or Addendum), and the page number.
- Avoid typos. Do everything within your power to make sure they don't happen. If they do happen, and you see one or two them after the application is submitted, do everything within your power not to throw yourself on the bed and cry or to jump off a bridge.[33]
- Don't send School A's personal statement to School B. Nothing you can do about that one once it's done. It's so embarrassing, and it happens all the time.
- Print out each application and check it before submitting it. Ask someone else to check it also.
- Avoid submitting things late at night. This is when mistakes happen. If you're exhausted, wait until the next day to submit the application. You only get one shot, so make sure it's perfect.

Remember, except in extreme circumstances, waiting a day won't make a difference, but a mistake in your application could make all the difference.

---

[33] For example, I wanted to jump off a bridge after finding errors in the first edition of this book. This was one reason why I decided to re-write it. Now, I will refrain from jumping off a bridge when you contact me to point out the typos in this version of the book.

CHAPTER 14

CHOOSING A LAW SCHOOL

How Should I Choose Where to Apply?

There are three kinds of law school applicants:

1. Those who are geographically tied to a region;
2. Those who are hunting for the best law school that will take them;
3. Those who are looking for the best value.

In my opinion, there aren't enough applicants who fall into category #3, so I'm going to start by addressing how those applicants should choose law schools. First, once you have your LSAT and GPA, look for schools where your numbers place you near the 75th percentile of admitted students. You can find this information on school websites or search for schools using the LSAC Admission Calculator.[34] Some of you will not be able to help yourselves: you will have to reach out to law school discussion forums for information about where people get in.

---

[34] https://officialguide.lsac.org/release/OfficialGuide_Default.aspx

But remember that this is self-selecting and really only fuels paranoia.[35]

Don't assume public schools will be the best deal. After all, out-of-state tuition can be astronomical, and the better scholarships might come from private universities because they can be more flexible in what they offer to you (particularly as an out-of-state applicant).

People who fall into category #1 have the easiest time choosing schools to apply to because there may be only one or two schools in their city. In this case, you want to make friends with the admission offices at the schools where you plan to apply. Make sure they know you and make sure you attend events, visit the campus, and listen to whatever advice they give to you. Personal connection will matter, especially if your numbers are marginal.

Suggestions for people willing to go almost anywhere in the country and who are less concerned with the cost of law school:

First, cast a wide net. There is no magic number of schools to apply to for one simple reason—it does no good for me to tell you to apply to 15 law schools if 10 of them are schools you have no hope of getting into. It's important to put schools into categories. Pick some schools where they take 15% or fewer of people with your numbers. These are your reach schools. (A school that never takes anyone with your numbers is not a reach school—it's a waste of an application.) If you have good soft factors, you should keep your options open by going heavy on

---

[35] Regarding Lawschoolpredictor.com and LawSchoolNumbers.com, one of my clients said, "LSP said I was a 'deny' at both Duke and NYU and was wrong on both."

the reach schools. They can even be more than half of your total applications.

Most of your schools list should be mid-range schools. That means that your numbers fall between the 25th and 75th percentiles for those schools. Some people within this range are admitted, and some aren't. This is where your brilliant personal statement, optional essays, resume, letters of recommendation, and soft factors come in to play.

It's always good to pick 2 to 4 safety schools. However, if you have problems in your application like an arrest or two or some other character and fitness issue of significance or some other significant weakness (like a downward trend with grades or an unimpressive resume), then you need to go heavy on the safety schools; these should be the bulk of your application list.

Except for the person who knows that moving is not a possibility, I like my clients to keep their options open. Over ten years as a law school admission consultant, I have seen people change their minds dramatically over the 6 to 9 months that they are deciding where to apply until the time when they have to choose where to attend. At first, people tend to think rankings are most important. And even if someone sticks to this philosophy, when the new rankings are released (right before deposit deadlines), the order of preference can change (which is pretty lame, if you ask me).[36] I see that scholarships become more important to people as they get closer to actually taking out loans in the amount of a mortgage. Also, people might enter into serious relationships or family issues arise that make a certain location especially appealing. This is why I think all

---

[36] Law schools don't change significantly from year to year, but *U.S.News and World Report* has to change the rankings or no one would buy their magazine or blog or tweet about the rankings.

applicants should apply to schools that (1) are near a place they consider home; (2) are in a place where they would be happy living their lives and pursuing their careers; (3) are reasonably priced; or (4) would be their dream to attend. If you cover all of these bases while balancing your reach/mid-range/safety positioning, you should end up with an array of good choices to make no matter where life might take you between the time you apply and the time when you have to commit to a school.

For those of you thinking that none of this applies to you because you want to go to law school only if you can get into Yale, Harvard, or Stanford, my first question is, "Do you really want to go to law school or are you looking for a brand name stamped across your tushy?" My second question is, "Do you have what it takes?" It amazes me how many calls I get from people with mediocre credentials who feel they are special, and they will be the person Harvard takes with a 148 and a 3.2. (It's not going to happen except for that one person who accomplishes the truly spectacular (solving the problems of the Middle East, for example) and then decides to apply to law school.) If you have an LSAT score into the 170s and a 3.9 GPA from a very good school, you've written a thesis, run a non-profit (or for-profit for that matter), and have a lot of great stuff going for you, then you're a great candidate for Harvard-Yale-Stanford. If this is you, then that's great. Just apply to these three (but most people in this category are humble enough to think they need to apply to at least the top ten law schools). I have a client this year who fell into this category—a 175, a 3.9 from one of these three schools as an undergrad, and meaningful professional experience for two years in addition to a pattern of community service and leadership. I told her she needed to apply only to these three (because scholarships were not important to her), but most of you need to spread your wings and give yourself more chances to succeed.

If you fall into category 2 or 3, your schools list will inevitably grow as you progress through the cycle because schools will throw application fee waivers at your feet. You will get an e-mail from Cornell or some other dream school offering you a free application and you will think, "Me! They want ME!" But they don't *necessarily*. In addition to wanting the best students, they want to keep their application numbers high so they can keep their acceptance rates low. If you were planning to apply to that school anyway, please go ahead and do so. Make sure they know you were going to apply anyway and you have a high level of interest so that they don't put you in the waitlist pile because they think you applied only because of the fee waiver.

How Do I Choose Where to Attend?

Once you've been admitted, the real fun begins. You thought waiting for decisions was hard; this is the agonizing part. There are three main criteria to consider:

1. Reputation
2. Location
3. Cost

The order of importance of these three varies based on which category of applicant you decided you were at the beginning of this chapter. I wrote an entire book about what lawyers think is important in choosing a law school, so if you are at this phase of the process, it's time to read *The Law School Decision Game*.

In this book's previous edition of this chapter, I wrote the following: "*What's Important in a Law School? JOBS. It's* that simple. You must consider which school will give you the most access to jobs." There are two ways to choose a law school around jobs: (1) you can go for the jobs that care about the brand name of the school you attend, or (2) you can choose a law school located in the city where you hope to build your law career.

Remember that most law school graduates aren't working in glamorous international law, jet-setting, foreign-policy setting careers. There is a lot of glamour, I think, in being a criminal defense attorney whose office resembles a shoe-box and whose suits are ten years old. But these two attorneys may or may not have gone to different law schools. It's more likely, however, that they both went to Harvard than that they both went to Western New England School of Law (both in Massachusetts). Why? Because the legal profession's bread and butter doesn't need to go to Harvard to do their jobs. But the upper echelon, elite positions are not easily accessible to graduates of lower-ranked law schools. I like to be polite and call them "regional" law schools because most of them are perfectly wonderful places to go if you plan to be a personal injury, civil rights, criminal defense, insurance defense, family law, or trusts and estates attorney. These are the attorneys that people and companies need for their everyday problems. This is real, roll-up-your-sleeves law. But it's not what most people have visions of doing when they are taking the LSAT. Going to a lower-ranked school absolutely will preclude you from clerking for the Supreme Court and becoming a law professor; but, if you are at the top of your class at a lower-ranked school, you will probably still have access to clerkships and Big Law positions to some degree.

In *The Law School Decision Game*, I interviewed 250 lawyers about their law school decisions, their careers, and the money they make. But at the risk of being repetitive, I am going to repeat the main points here because I fear too many of you will be overly idealistic and refuse to read that book, just hoping/wishing/praying everything will work out for you. Law practice is demanding. The hours are long. And you'll be doing well just by making $100,000 a year, and that's after many years of hard work.

To find the school that will best prepare you and where you will be happiest, I suggest that you visit as many law schools as you can. One of my former clients said,

> "I visited 12 schools during my application process, and through that I got a much better feel for each place than I ever could have via websites, forums, and brochures. Even among peer schools there's a huge range of experiences you can have. Don't let someone tell you what a school is like. Go see it, spend the day there, get separated from the guided tour, talk to students, and try to imagine spending the next three years in that setting. If you can, great. If not, better to waste a day figuring that out now."

Other former clients of mine had this to add:

- "Either go to the best school you get into or the school that gives you a full ride. Having Columbia Law on my resume helped me more with my job search than I could have imagined. On the other hand, if I had no debt I probably wouldn't have been as stressed." (E.K., Columbia Law student)
- "Frankly, with the current economy and job prospects for law grads, my advice to people has been "Go T-14 or Go for free." If you go that path, you are much more likely to either (a) have a job at graduation; or

(b) not have debt at graduation. I'm not sure right now that I would pick Fordham over the option to attend Brooklyn for free. Clearly, Fordham was the best place for me (with strong IP and 8 blocks from my apartment), but I am a unicorn who got an in-house job in IP which is basically unheard of. I think "T-14 or free" really applies to those who don't necessarily know what kind of law they want to practice. A school with specific strengths/alumni networks won't necessarily help someone who doesn't realize until 3L what practice areas excite them." (Sarah Yood, Fordham Law graduate)

- "My advice on choosing a law school would be to balance job prospects with debt level. I think limiting debt is incredibly important. Even if you get Big Law, going to law school at full cost can mean debt hanging over your head for years (and limiting what you are able to do in life). If you don't want Big Law (and excluding career paths like academia), then I think it only makes sense to try and limit debt as much as possible, unless you want to do public interest and you can go to a school with a good LRAP (Loan Repayment Assistance Program) and give good public interest connections. Also, it's vital to make sure the school you are considering can actually give you a decent shot at a legal job. The sad thing is, especially in this economy, there are a ton of law schools that might just waste three years of your life and leave you only in a worse position than when you started law schools." (Brian Bah, University of Texas School of Law)

- Even lower-ranked schools can have great alumni networks. "I recognized that real-world experience and training was highly important because I knew prior to law school that I wanted to be a litigator. I chose Southwestern Law School because it had a trial-focused curriculum and an honors program in trial advocacy. The trial experience I obtained during law school made me a prime candidate for a post-graduate fellowship with the Los Angeles Chapter of the American Board of Trial Advocates, and this fellowship placed me in firms and allowed me to meet seasoned attorneys and some of the best litigators in the country. The alumni network was very interested in hiring the school's graduates. Ultimately, I got my current position because an alumnus of my law school from my fellowship referred me to a colleague in need of a new associate." (Ashlee Clark, Graduate of Southwestern Law School)

This is another time when discussion forums can be an easy resource but a destructive force in your decision making. One of my really savvy former clients (now a 1L at New York University Law School), who has spent a lot more time than I have on Top-Law-Schools.com, has the following take on it: "Posters with five-digit post counts create elaborate models to determine which schools are better than other schools, and people repeat their conclusions as gospel even though they have absolutely no clue where the models or data sets come from, or what the potential weaknesses could be. Yes, Virginia is a better bet than George Washington for almost everything, and Carolina will always beat Campbell, but a slavish devotion to conventional wisdom match obscures certain things that make certain schools look stronger or weaker than others when they actually aren't. Top-Law-Schools.com still talks dozens of snow-hating "Empire State of Mind," "California Dreamin,'" and "GeorgeTTTown" admits into moving to Ithaca, Ann Arbor, or Chicago every year. It's sad."

What Should I Worry About?

- *Don't Follow Rankings Blindly.* This year's #21 and #17 could reverse next year, and then you'd feel dumb for choosing one because it was top 20. By the time you graduate from law school, either school could be a Top 14 or a Top 30.

- *Watch out for the for-profit law schools.* (One of my former clients calls them "soul-sucking for-profit scam-schools.") These are often the schools with high rates of 1Ls who don't make it through the first year. Schools that take a lot of people with low numbers are giving them a chance to succeed, but these applicants don't always make it. Sometimes low numbers really do show a person's potential for succeeding in law school.

- *Be true to yourself.* Don't choose a school because other people will be impressed by it or because people know the school's football program. This is a decision you'll have to live with so make a choice that feels right to you. If you are not happy with any of your choices, consider re-applying to law school and including different schools, improving your credentials and/ or materials, and trying again. Don't make a good short-term decision at the expense of a much better long-term decision.

- *Don't count on being able to transfer after your first year.* Assume when you start at a law school that this is the law school you will graduate from. If you end up excelling during your first year (top 20% or above), then you can think about transferring to a different law school. But remember that this isn't so easy when everyone is bright, motivated, vying for the same goal of being at the top of the class.

- *Don't just look at the self-reported employment number if you're looking at job statistics and then call it a day.* Look into whether graduates are in jobs that require J.D.s, whether the law school is hiring its own graduates to boost the numbers, and check out www.lawschooltransparency.com.

CHAPTER 15

INTERVIEWS

Will I Have to Interview with Law Schools?

MOST law schools do not interview applicants. There are simply too many applicants to handle this. A few law schools encourage interviews as part of their process (see Category #2, "Strongly Suggested Interviews" below).

There are three kinds of "interviews" in the law school admission process:

1. *Informal:* You make an appointment with the admission office, and you do not call it an interview but you do get (very often) one-on-one face time with someone who is a decision-maker. From your end, the purpose is to become more than just a paper application so they can put a face to the name and you can make a favorable impression, address any perceived weaknesses, express your interest in the school, and gain advice about how to move forward.

2. *Strongly Suggested:* Northwestern and Vanderbilt strongly suggest applicants sign up for an interview, either on campus or with an alumna in your

hometown. One of my clients said this about her experience, "I met with an alum (who seemed to be in his mid- to late-60s) and he pretty much just asked me what my interest in Vanderbilt was and then asked me specific questions that he had from looking at my resume." (She was admitted with a high 150s LSAT score.) My clients who interview on campus with someone in the admissions office at Northwestern find it very straightforward. The interviewer has seen the applicant's resume and asks about the experiences there.

3. *Requested:* Harvard, as has Georgetown, has been interviewing people via Skype by invitation only. All of my clients who have done the Harvard Skype interview this year received admission offers within four weeks of their interview. This is really a check to make sure you're not a crazy person, that you are who you say you are, and that you have some social skills. One of my clients told me that this interview felt a bit like she was being grilled on her academic background and that the 20-minute timeframe was strictly adhered to. She was pretty worried about how it went, but in the end she was admitted. She had a completely different experience with the Chicago Skype interview (where she was also later admitted and given a full scholarship): this interview was personable, less pressured, and not limited to her resume. Really, your interview will depend on who conducts it, but you need to be prepared for any of these possibilities. One of my clients who had Skype interviews at both Chicago and Georgetown said he quickly realized the interviewer

was not there to trick him, but that they generally wanted to know him better.

Georgetown has also been holding group interviews by invitation. For example, one of my clients attended a group interview in the Bay Area for applicants from Berkeley and Stanford. This was a completely different ball game: the participants were given two law examples of law school applicants and asked whom to admit! It was a test of the ability to think on your feet, to lead without being dominating, and to support your stance.

Southwestern Law has been requesting that people take the time to interview with alumni in order to be considered for scholarships. University of Chicago and other schools have been holding Skype interviews with "held" and "waitlisted" applicants.

Some select scholarships involve interviews; usually these are public interest scholarships. One of my clients interviewed for a scholarship at the University of Pennsylvania Law School and the panel included four people, including two practicing public interest lawyers. They asked about her interest in the program and her goals, and they inquired more specifically into the area of public interest law that she hoped to practice. The school paid for part of her expenses for travel to the interview.

CHAPTER 16

WAITLISTS, DEFERRALS, HOLDS, AND RESERVE LISTS

What Do I Do Now That I Am on a Waiting List?

WHEN a client calls me, distraught that he has been wait-listed, I say, "Congratulations!" He then sounds very confused. On a waiting list, you are still in the running. On a waiting list, you still have some control over your future. On a waiting list, you can get into your dream law school. That's why I say "Congratulations!" A waiting list means hope! (As does a "held" and "reserve" decision, by the way.)

However, it also implies that you need to get used to waiting. Because this is the best way to get into a reach law school, you need to stay motivated. "The single best piece of advice I can give any applicant is to treat the admissions cycle as something that ends in August, not in March," said one of my former clients who applied to 16 law schools, was accepted at 6 and rejected at one. "This was somewhat frustrating, but Ann was optimistic. My GPA wasn't what the top schools wanted, but I had a compelling story to tell and some interesting soft factors that she felt would tip the balance. I kept in regular contact with a number of admission offices, and jumped through every hoop I was asked to. I even visited some of the schools in person, which was useful in helping me replace the *U.S.News* rankings with my own personal fit rankings. I managed to get off two lists in April (and still got a partial scholarship to one of the schools). I signed a lease and moved to Durham to attend Duke when I was accepted to NYU off the waiting list in July. I visited NYU and decided to go. It was chaotic but in the end it's the best place for me."

He also had this to say: "Looking back, it's clear to me how much of a blessing a waitlist can be. If I hadn't made the decision to aggressively pursue my waitlists way back in March, I would either be fretting about my employment prospects or absolutely miserable at a school where I didn't fit in. I know a lot of people at NYU who were admitted from the waitlist and nobody cares—not our classmates, not our professors, not the recruiters, and certainly not our exams. If you get wait-listed somewhere and you want to go there, keep fighting for it until the last day of Orientation. You never know what might happen."

When and How Should I Pursue a School Where I Am on the Wait List?

Most law schools don't even think about the people on their waiting list until after they have the first deposits from the people they've admitted. It is only after they see how those numbers come back that they start to evaluate their waitlisted applicants.

When a law school starts to review a waiting list to admit people, they may have specific needs. For example, if more women sent deposits than men they may need to balance out the class this way. If the LSAT numbers for the entering class are looking strong but the GPAs are looking lackluster, they may go to people with strong GPAs. They might see that they have too many people from a certain undergrad school and not enough from another, or by geographic region, or there is room to expand on ethnic diversity. These are all considerations when deciding who will be admitted.

And, within each of these categories that need to be filled, the Dean of Admissions is thinking, "Who do I like? Whose day do I want to make?" After all, this is one of the most fun things an admission officer gets to do. I want to call someone who I know is going to be very happy to hear from me. I get to be a hero today! So who do I call? That nice kid who has been in touch with me for six months! The guy who works down the street as a paralegal! The young woman who traveled from Ohio to visit the law school! This is where making an effort makes all the difference. After all, I don't want to have to make 5 calls to get someone who is happy to hear from me. I want the person who is the sure thing, because what I don't want is to admit someone at this point in the year who is not going to attend. Remember, law schools try to keep their acceptance rates low (and matriculation rates high) due to the way they are ranked, so they do not want to extend offers to 100 people on the waiting list and simply hope that 22 accept: they want to make only 22 calls to fill 22 spots.

If you do absolutely nothing beyond accepting your place on the waiting list, you will not get into the law school. That's all there is to it. You must go above and beyond. You must launch your campaign to get in. If this chapter is more pep talk than tips, it's because I've seen too many people discouraged by a wait list decision when they should be encouraged by it. Just this week, I had a client tell me that he wasn't going to pursue the waiting list at Catholic or American because he might not hear back until August and he didn't want to move in August. "Hello?" I said. "It's only March! Campaign now! Hang in there now! If you still haven't heard in July and you don't want to stay on the waiting list then, ok. But you could hear something in May or June if you campaign now." People give up too soon. Also, people assume there will be no scholarship offers from schools where they are admitted off the waiting list. This used to be the case, but in recent years this has changed and more schools are reserving (or redistributing) scholarship funds after deposit deadlines to both admitted students and those who are newly admitted from the waiting list. (See Chapter 18, "Scholarships.")

Of course, I've had clients receive calls from their top choice law school while sitting in Orientation at their second choice law school. Sometimes this happens, and it can be an awesome (if stressful) thing. But most waitlist news comes in plenty of time for you to enter into a lease and buy books.

Here is a schedule of things to do when you are waitlisted:

- Immediately and enthusiastically accept a place on the waiting list. Refrain from immediately bombarding the law school with letters and additional information, especially if you get your wait list notification before March.

- Schedule a campus tour and visit if you have not already done so and if it is economically feasible. If you live in the same city or state and haven't visited, the school isn't going to think you're very interested in attending. Does visiting really help? People ask me that all the time. I had a client who was absolutely dying to go to law school, and he didn't care where so long as he could practice law one day. He flew himself across the country to visit Thomas Jefferson School of Law where he was waitlisted, even though he'd been told he would have only ten minutes with the assistant director of admissions. The ten minutes turned into an hour, and two days later he was admitted.

- During your visit, try to get some face-time (*don't ask for an interview!*) with an admission counselor/officer. Ask about the waiting list and what they recommend in terms of keeping in touch, and then follow that to the "T." Talk to everyone you meet, ask students about their experiences at the law school, ask them what they did if they were waitlisted, introduce yourself to the professor whose class you are visiting, and follow up by writing thank-you notes (or e-mails) to each of them.

- Immediately after the deposit deadlines (since there is sometimes more than one) follow up with a letter expressing your interest in attending the law school—be specific!

- As you receive new (superb) grades, and/or honors, and/or promotions at work, or take on a new job or leadership position, e-mail the admissions office with the news.

- Refrain from stalking the admissions office. Keep in touch every month until deposit deadlines have passed, then maybe every 2 to 4 weeks depending on the vibe you are getting from the school and whether you have real updates to pass along.

- If you feel very confident in your ability to raise your LSAT score by more than 2 points, then consider a June retake. You would probably still be on the waiting list in June and improving your LSAT score could make the difference.
- Some law schools specifically invite you to submit additional essays, including Penn Law, Northwestern Law, Michigan State, and Southwestern. If you pass this opportunity by, the law school will assume you are not interested in attending.

Can I Send a Deposit to More Than One School?

It's very common that a school will have an April 1 or April 15 deposit deadline, particularly for scholarship recipients, and that you will not have heard back from other schools by then. You will need to send a deposit to secure your spot. If you end up getting into another school that you would prefer to attend, you simply lose your deposit. No biggie.

You can ask schools to extend these deadlines for a couple of weeks if you haven't yet had time to visit or if you are still waiting for a particular school's decision. As long as you ask nicely, the worst they can say is, "Sorry, no."

You may send deposits to more than one school with the caveat that the schools will know you have sent multiple deposits and can make you put up or shut up, at which point you'll have to withdraw from one of those schools (hence, spots opening up for waitlisted candidates at this time).

> LSAC provides participating law schools with periodic reports detailing the number of applicants who have submitted seat deposits or commitments at other participating schools, along with identification of those

other schools. Beginning May 15 of each year, these reports now include the names and LSAC account numbers for all candidates who have deposits/commitments at multiple participating schools.[37]

---

[37] www.lsac.org/jd/apply/whom-to-admit.asp

CHAPTER 17

TAKING TIME OFF BEFORE LAW SCHOOL

Should I Take Time Off Before Law School?

WHEN people first ask me this question, I think they usually mean, "Will law schools like me better if I take a year or two off before applying?" If your grades need to show another year of improvement and/or you need more time to prepare for the LSAT, absolutely there can be a benefit to your admission chances to wait a year. However, grades and LSAT being equal, there is no clear preference for an applicant who takes time off and one who goes to law school straight from college.[38]

Some of the benefits to taking time off include:

- The chance to show an upward trend in grades;
- Saving money for law school;
- Deciding what you want to do with your life/career;

---

[38] Even Northwestern Law, which spends a lot of time discussing the value of work experience in applicants, takes people straight out of college. However, *Yale Daily News* reported in 2011 that only 20 percent of the entering first year class at Yale Law School came straight from college. yaledailynews.com/blog/2011/gap-years-strengthen-law-school-plans/

- Taking classes and/or having jobs that will garner positive letters of recommendation.

Nathan Fox, a graduate of UC Hastings, told me a funny (but true!) story: "During my first semester, the most complaining came from the youngest members of my 1L section. They'd arrive for our first class at 11 a.m., drinking Starbucks and wearing hoodie sweatshirts and flip flops and spend 15 minutes whining to each other about how hard and stressful law school was. It was pretty amusing to those of us who had held real jobs before. You know, with bosses. And dress codes. And days that start before lunchtime."

Having professional experience can also help you manage your time during law school. According to Nathan, "Law school can easily overrun your life, if you let it. I'd frequently see the 21-year olds having frantic, unproductive study groups at 11 p.m. However, one of my friends drew a box around law school and dominated. He was a bit older, with real-world experience, and he simply turned law school into a 40-hour, Monday-Friday work week. He never took his books home once during the entire 1L year. He'd show up at 9 a.m. every day, even if he only had one class in the afternoon. When he wasn't in class, he was in the library reading. He left every day at 5 p.m., slamming his books in his locker. Unsurprisingly, he got awesome grades. It was a classy way to do it."

One of my clients was admitted to Yale Law School and was all set to go. Instead, she deferred admission for a year and took a job as a paralegal in a civil rights firm. She sees immense value in this experience. "I am learning how the law is actually practiced, how litigators live their lives, and both the excitement and challenges that come from being a practicing lawyer.

This experience will guide my decisions in law school (what kinds of clinics I do, what kind of internships I apply for) and is giving me a much clearer sense of what I want to do with my law degree. I feel like I am preempting the shell shock that comes from transitioning into the real world of lawyering after law school and gaining real-world experience you just can't get as a 1L," she said.

"If you are looking to be at a law firm, it is really great to take a year or two off before law school and work at a big firm as a paralegal or legal assistant so that you already have your foot in the door," said a client currently attending Columbia Law School. Another client told me "You can't know if yet more school (and debt) is the right choice unless you experience life outside of school."

"Having work experience can be incredibly helpful during OCI (On-Campus Interviews)," according to Rebecca Sivitz, a graduate of the University of Pennsylvania Law School.

And, let's be honest, sometimes you just need a break. One of my clients said, "Taking time off was one of the best decisions I've ever made; I'm so glad I did it. By my senior year, I was feeling burned out and the prospect of going straight to three years of law school felt daunting. I was also scared that if I went directly to law school then I would be putting myself on this track (of going to law school and working super hard, then having some crazy job during both summers, and then getting a job and working crazy hours) that I wouldn't be able to get off of. So, mentally, it was really good for me to pause things and have a year to take a breath. I also used this year to volunteer and travel, and got the experience of being a young professional in a city where I had previously only been a full-time student. I also used the time I've had to really think about what I might want to do with my law degree and how I can set myself up to do that, which allows me to take into consideration the specific programs and tracks that various law schools have. Therefore, I feel I will be making a much more informed decision than I would have made if I had applied last year, while I was still in school. This year has also been really good for me personally, because last year I felt that I wasn't ready to leave New Orleans, and I think that I've matured this year and gotten some perspective, and that I will be able to leave if I choose to."

Should I Get a Paralegal Certificate during My Time Off from School?

A paralegal certificate is not a prerequisite for working as a paralegal. Law schools won't place a lot of stock in your high grades in paralegal school, either. But taking the initiative to do a one-year program can be helpful if you are trying to demonstrate a real interest in law and you are trying to garner additional letters of recommendation. However, make sure you can afford the paralegal certificate; it's not worth taking out loans unless you intend to work as a paralegal for several years.

CHAPTER 18

SCHOLARSHIPS

How Do I Get a Scholarship to Law School?

MOST scholarships are given based on merit alone; there is no separate application. A few schools use separate scholarship applications for public interest scholarships or very focused (and very prestigious) opportunities, but most schools will let you know about scholarship offers at the same time (or shortly after) they offer you admission. You can guess which schools will offer you scholarships based on how competitive your numbers are; obviously, schools use scholarships to motivate people with higher numbers to attend. They are also used by lower-ranked schools more liberally to encourage people to attend, period.

What Should I Know about Law School Scholarships?

Scholarships range in amount from approximately, $5,000 to $40,000 per year. It's important to look at the renewability criteria for any scholarship and ask about the likelihood of it being renewed. Is the required GPA for keeping the scholarship a 2.3 or is a 3.3? A 3.3 might sound like a low threshold by undergraduate standards, but in law school that places you in the top third of your class. You can't assume that because you are a "merit scholarship" recipient that you would be in the top third of your law school class. You should ask a law school what percentage of scholarship recipients end up keeping them after the first year of law school.

You may get a scholarship even if you are pulled off a waiting list because (1) more funds are available because of people who turned down their spots in the class, and (2) because law schools want to seal the deal and solidify their classes.

How Do I Negotiate a Bigger Scholarship?

You can negotiate scholarships, but you need to be gentle about it and have a plan. Schools are sensitive to being used: they know you might be asking for more money from them simply to get another school to pony up more.

When negotiating scholarships, here are some important things to keep in mind:

- *You want to demonstrate your strong interest in the school.* It's even better if you can say that an increased scholarship offer would seal the deal, and you would immediately send in a deposit and/or withdraw all other applications, etc. "I got Penn up from a "final offer" by saying that I'd consider it but if they could offer me $X more, then I'd commit immediately," said one of my former clients.
- *It's good to have a specific number in mind.* Will $2,500 more really make a difference for you? Or would you need a certain amount because a similarly ranked law school in your home town would allow you to live at home and save money?
- *Present the school with one or two select scholarship offers.*

Use offers from schools that are similarly ranked and similarly situated or even better—ranked higher.

- *Be polite about it.* Don't sound arrogant, demanding, or entitled. I had a client who sent a pretty obnoxious e-mail to UCLA (without running it past me first!) about the great offers Duke and University of Southern California gave him, and the Dean at UCLA basically told him, "Well, then, good luck at Duke or USC." Then my client was in a panic because UCLA really was one of his top choices. (Don't worry, I talked him through fixing the problem, but trust me that this isn't a situation you want to find yourself in.)
- *Don't make it a game.* If the scholarship (or increase) really wouldn't make the difference in getting you to attend, then refrain from making it a game. If law schools smell that, they will tear you apart.
- *Don't exaggerate your offers from other schools.* Law schools will check their facts. Wake Forest will call William and Mary and ask, "Did you really give Joe Smith $30,000 a year?"

CHAPTER 19

TRANSFERRING LAW SCHOOLS

Can I Change Law Schools After My First Year?

AFTER your first year of law school, you may be eligible to transfer to another law school. This is generally a one-shot only deal. Reasons for transferring include attending a school with better job opportunities and/or attending a school closer to home. Before you think to yourself, "Aha! I'll go to whatever school I can get into and then transfer after my first year," think again. Transferring (especially to top-ranked law schools) is highly competitive. You should *never* select a law school with the intention of transferring after the first year; doing so will only set you up for disappointment and make it more likely that you will become one of those disgruntled 3Ls lining up to sue your law school.

However, it's good to know that *if* you do well, and *if* you prove during your 1L year that your GPA and LSAT score did not accurately predict your performance, you will have the option to transfer to a more prestigious school. Why does this work? Because law schools don't have to report your LSAT and GPA to the ABA: it doesn't count against their ranking. Of course, they won't be throwing scholarships at you to recruit you either. You get to attend the "better" law school, and they get to charge you full tuition (to help cover the cost of those 1L recruiting scholarships they had to give out).

What Do I Need to Do to Transfer?

You will be evaluated based on your performance during your first year of law school and the quality of law school you attended. Your grades and class rank will be the deciding factors at this point; the higher up the rankings you want to jump, the higher up your class rank and the law school's caliber need to be in order to be considered.

Just being in the top 30% of your class at a regional law school won't get you a spot at Georgetown (the most popular place to transfer based on the number of transfers they take and their consistent Top-14 ranking). But being in the top 5 percent at your Top 100 school might just get you there. I've had clients transfer from Golden Gate to William and Mary (had a 3.0 then a 3.5 second semester), from Catholic, Chicago Kent, and University of San Francisco to Georgetown (top 5 percent), from George Mason to Northwestern (#2 in his class), from Touro to Cardozo (top 10 percent), from Cardozo to Columbia (#3 in his class), and from Southwestern to University of Southern California (top 10 percent). I also had a client from New York University who was admitted as a transfer to both Stanford and Harvard. It can be very hard to predict where you might be admitted because law schools do not report where they take transfers from or the credentials of their transfer students.

In addition to a ranking high in your class, you will need a letter of recommendation from a law school faculty member and a personal statement that addresses the reasons why you want to transfer.

Are there Downsides to Transferring?

The transfer process happens at two times of the year. A handful of schools will take transfers as Early Decision transfers after first semester grades are released, as in the case of Georgetown and University of Southern California. For the rest, transfer applications are submitted when first year grades are received, and decisions are made very quickly. Therefore, you have just a quick 2- to 4-week turnaround where admission decisions are reached and you have to make a decision. Sounds great, but there is a downside: you'll need to pick up and move. This isn't so hard when you are going from Catholic to Georgetown or Cardozo to Columbia, but a cross-country move at the last minute can be traumatic. You'll also be saying goodbye to the friends you've made and jumping in to a place where people already bonded during their first year. You may have a hard time with on-campus interviews for your 2L summer, and you may have to write a law review article on very short notice to try to earn a spot on a law journal. You may even have to wait until your 2L summer to try to earn a spot on the journal.

CHAPTER 20

HIRING A LAW SCHOOL ADMISSION CONSULTANT

What Is a Law School Admission Consultant?[39]

A good consultant gives you an added layer of guidance and confidence by lending his or her expertise and talents to build the strength of your application materials. The consultant does this by helping make sure your written materials are as strong as they can be, that you are applying to the right schools in the right way, and that you are making good decisions throughout the admission cycle. Yes, you may have a parent or friend who applied to law school, and he or she may be familiar with the process, but a law school admission consultant should have been through this process hundreds or even thousands of times, and you will get the benefit of all that experience.

---

[39] Bias alert: Yes, I am a law school admission consultant. I get it: I have something at stake here. However, I believe in what I do. I believe I am helping people create the best possible futures for themselves. I believe I help people make good, well-informed decisions. I am proud of the work I have done to help my clients over the past (almost) decade, and I believe that people who take advantage of what a law school admission consultant has to offer are in the best possible position to reach their goals.

You may just want someone with law school admission experience to give you feedback on a draft of your personal statement or on your addendum, or you may want someone who will hold your hand and guide you through each decision, each application, each essay, waitlist campaign, scholarship negotiation, and deposit deadline. Most consultants are set up to help you with as much or as little as you would like help with.

A lot of parents are the ones to reach out to me: they want to equip their (adult) children with every possible advantage. They also want to make sure someone is looking over their child's shoulder and helping to move things forward when life gets in the way and stalls the process for their active twenty-something. Often, and perhaps secretly, they want to remove themselves from the process to preserve the relationship with their child. Having a law school admission consultant work with their child allows them to become a supporter from the sidelines rather than the coach.

Why Does Anyone Need a Law School Admission Consultant?

Newsflash: I do not believe everyone needs a law school admission consultant. In fact, if it's a question of getting help with your LSAT prep or help from an admission consultant, I will choose LSAT prep for you 9 out of 10 times (especially if you are one of the people who takes advantage of the free initial consultation I offer through my website and your highest LSAT score is a 132). In addition, there are some undergraduate schools that have effective and helpful pre-law advisors. They won't be able to be as hands-on as a consultant, but they will generally look at final drafts of materials and help you with some strategy. Pre-law advisors are often over-worked, under-paid, and sometimes under-trained. Quite a few have attended my lectures at universities through the years, and I always enjoy answering their questions and speaking with them.

Law school applicants who benefit most from working with a consultant include:

- Those with a weakness in their application, such as a low GPA, poor LSAT score, and/or a character and fitness issue;
- People who do not have access to lawyers or pre-law advisors (NON-TRADITIONAL applicants);
- Highly motivated applicants who want to make the process as easy and efficient as possible and maximize their chances of getting into the best possible law schools;[40]
- People who want to save time: instead of scouring the web every time a question arises, they want someone they can call;
- Someone who wants a timeline set up for them, a method of accountability and motivation, and feedback catered specifically to their unique situation;
- People looking for an objective perspective from someone who is not a family member, a friend, or a lawyer who thinks she knows what she is talking about;
- People re-applying to law school who aren't quite sure

---

[40] One of my clients said, "I think that even really strong applicants can benefit from admissions consultants. They provide value to even highly competitive applicants by helping them put together an amazing package that makes them more likely to be considered for scholarship money. Also, hiring a consultant ensures you don't accidentally raise red flags or make foolish mistakes."

what went wrong the first time and they don't want to repeat their mistakes;

- INTERNATIONAL students who aren't familiar with the system of U.S. education and are feeling insecure about writing a personal essay.

What Should I Consider Before Hiring a Law School Admission Consultant?

Again, this will appear to be somewhat self-serving because I am hoping you drop the book right now, call me,[41] and ask me these questions, but I'm hoping my suggestions will be helpful to you as you call around.

A few things to consider before hiring a consultant:

- Is the consultant a law school specialist or does he or she also help people with college and graduate school applications? Is he or she also a practicing attorney who is doing consulting on the side?
- Has the consultant been a decision-maker for a law school admission office?
- Will you be working directly with the consultant or with his or her employees?
- What are the preferred methods of contact?
- Has the consultant worked with people applying to the law schools you hope to attend?
- How quickly will e-mails and phone calls be answered and how quickly will drafts of documents be turned around?

---

[41] Nathan Fox says I should put my phone number here, but I think it's too cheesy. Here's the compromise: visit my website at www.lawschoolexpert.com and fill out a form so that I can contact you.

- Is the consultant available during hours that are convenient for you?
- Is the consultant willing to put you in touch with references who are current or former clients with goals and credentials similar to yours?
- Why did the person become an admission consultant? Did he or she fail the bar exam or have trouble finding employment as a practicing attorney?
- How long has he or she been a law school admission consultant and how many people has the consultant helped?[42]
- Look out for consultants who offer too much, "I have a friend who hired a consultant who promised that they could use their connections to lobby for them, and they didn't, and it was pretty much a scam," said one graduate of a Top 14 school.

---

[42] A lot of people ask me how many people I'm working with at once, but it's not exactly the right question. What really matters is responsiveness, availability, and experience. The number of clients I've helped in the past is a better indicator of my experience than the number I am currently working with, and the fact that I aim to return calls and e-mails within a few hours and documents within 24 hours is more helpful information than the number of people I'm working with on a particular day or during a particular month.

CHAPTER 21

LAW SCHOOL ADVICE

What Should I Know Before Going to Law School?

I could (and did!) write a whole book on this subject.[43]

- You need to know that law school is right for you, that you can afford a law degree (now and in the future), and the sacrifices you will be making in the process.
- You need to know what to expect from the law school experience. You need to know what's going to be demanded of you in the classroom, and what you should be putting on your resume in terms of activities at the law school.
- You need to be ready to network to find a job. The best thing you could do right now for yourself (whether you end up going to law school or not) is to learn how to network effectively, how to reach out to people, make contacts, and learn about opportunities as they arise. This is the only way to become a successful professional. Your time starts now.

---

[43] See *The Law School Decision Game: A Playbook for Prospective Lawyers*

There is so much to say about gearing up to be successful in law school. Some people will give you a list of books to read that you can't understand; some will recommend a law school preparation course. I suggest reading interesting things (regardless of whether they have to do with the law) and practicing meeting new people and making connections, and then just relax so you are ready to work when law school starts.

When I asked my Facebook friends for tips and advice for people starting law school, their comments really fell into three categories: academic performance, professors, and law journals. I've included some of their comments below.

Academic Performance

> "As someone who had wanted to go to law school for a long time, the experience I have had thus far was surprising. I didn't excel (despite having a near perfect undergraduate GPA). I have gotten Bs and a B- or two and have had a harder time finding my place than I anticipated. A lot of it has had to do with my attitude and in some part the bad advice I got before going to law school.

> 1. *The worst piece of advice that I got was that you don't learn how to be a lawyer in law school.* Having been told this over and over again, I went into law school with a horrible attitude of thinking, "These people have nothing to teach me, so why pay attention?" and I really missed a lot of the substantive law I should have absorbed in my first year. During my second year, I really paid attention and, lo and behold, I really

know about corporations now, etc. So, to sum up, you do learn law in law school, and it is important.

2. *The second worst piece of advice I got was that no matter how hard you try, you won't do well; law school is too hard.* What a joke. As with anything in life, usually you get out of it what you put in. If you go into the experience already thinking that no matter how hard you work you won't get results, it really offers little motivation to try hard. The people who I watched bust their butts did really well. End of story.

3. *Someone else told me that grades don't matter and that I shouldn't do journal because it is boring.* Even if you aren't looking for that Big Law job, public inter-est work is still super competitive, and you need to have the best credentials possible. Unfortunately, the system still values grades and certain checkmarks on the resume: employers want to see grades and particu-lar activities. And networking during your first year is SUPER important.

   Some good advice that I received was that you really, really, really shouldn't go to law school until you are ready to put in the work it requires. Law school is the hardest thing I have ever done, and I am not sure even I was ready to take on that commitment."

                                        (E.K., Columbia Law School)

"Choose classes for 2L and 3L year wisely. Look at teacher evaluations, look to see if they have past exams and if those are in a format that you are good at, look at past grade distributions for that professor, talk to other law students about the class and the professor.

Most importantly, make sure you are interested in
the content. Don't take Wills and Estates just because
everyone else is doing it or because it's on the bar if
you think you will be bored to death in the class. It's
important not to fall into groupthink. There is not
one perfect way to study; you need to find out what
works best for you, even if that's different from what
others are doing. You need to think long and hard
about what you want your legal career to be, and talk
to professors and lawyers actually doing what you
want to do to see if your plans are realistic and attain-
able. This might be based on school, but there can
be this magnetic draw to Big Law and clerkships. If
that's what you want to do, that's fine. If you haven't
thought about it, then think about it. Don't compete
for top stuff just because it's the top stuff. Make sure
it's actually stuff you want."

(Brian Bah, University of Texas School of Law)

"It's impossible to predict how you will do in law school.
Being in the middle of a top 10 school doesn't necessarily translate to being #1 at a school ranked 100; there
are smart people at every school and other factors than
intelligence (like stress management) can impact where
you fall in a class."

(Rebecca Sivitz, graduate of the University
of Pennsylvania Law School)

Professors

"Making friends with a few professors will take you far
after law school. They're great people to get to know

because they are the ones with connections in the real world."

(Alyssa Tornberg, Quinnipiac Law)

"Go to office hours. Start going at the beginning of the semester and try to keep it up throughout. For some classes and some professors it's more helpful than others, but it's a great way to force yourself to dig deep in to the material to look for good questions, and it helps you find professors that you click with. This can be important when it comes to references for jobs and clerkships."

(Brian Bah, University of Texas School of Law)

Law Journals

The value of participating on a journal is widely debated, but if you want to work in Big Law, clerk for a judge, and/ or enter academia, then you're going to need to suffer through law review. Here is a smattering of comments from my former clients regarding their work on law journals:

- "I do not regret doing law review at all. It can be time consuming, but it's made me so much better at the *Bluebook* and editing in general." (Brian Bah, University of Texas School of Law)
- "Law review/journal isn't worth the one line on your resume. Almost everyone I know said it took up way too much time for little to nothing in return." (Alyssa Tornberg, Quinnipiac Law)
- "My specialized journal led to a job opportunity which included working on a SCOTUS case. Had I

not had the journal, I wouldn't have gotten the job!"
(Sara Yood, Fordham Law)

• "In Philly, and in pretty much the entire Delaware
Valley, I think being on law review is hugely helpful
(at least if you want to work at a firm—it might be a
different scenario for public interest or other areas).
I know that at my school, those of us with Big Law
internships lined up for the summer are on Law
Review or another journal. I was actually asked about
my case note topic in every interview. It definitely
takes a lot of time, but I haven't heard of anyone at my
school who regrets participating. Here, Law Review is
95 percent grade-ons and 5 percent write-ons, which
means that in addition to having the journal on your
resume, you're usually highly ranked in the class."
(Katie Hester, Villanova Law)

RESOURCES

Podcasts

- For more than 20 of my free podcasts on topics ranging from preparing for the LSAT to getting a job out of law school, choosing a law school to attend, writing a personal statement, and applying to law school, go to www.blogtalkradio.com/ann-levine.

Re: Getting into Law School

- *Officialguide.lsac.org* —all of the relevant data (including admission numbers) for every ABA Approved law school (this used to be published as a book but now is available only online).
- *How to Survive the First Year of Law School* (www.americanbar.org/content/dam/aba/migrated/lsd/membership/benefits/survive.authcheckdam.pdf).

LSAT Preparation

- Nextsteptestprep.com/lsatblog http://www.foxtestprep.com/lsat-blog/category/lsat-fundamentals.
- To pick up real LSAT practice tests as cheaply as

possible, check Amazon for the "Actual Official
LSAT" series:
http://www.amazon.com/s/
ref=nb_sb_noss?url=search-alias%3Daps&field-
keywords=actual%2C+official+LSAT.

- The Manhattan LSAT Forums www.manhattanlsat.
com/forums/.
The largest free online repository of high quality
LSAT answer explanations, and blog www.manhat-
tanlsat.com/blog.

- www.CambridgeIsat.com (download tests, practice
problems, and some explanations).

- www.Lsatblog.blogspot.com (read tips on specific
question types).

- www.Top-law-schools.com/forums (ask questions on
just about anything, but take all advice with caution
because you don't really know who is giving it).

SAMPLE RESUMES

THE following are three examples of drafts of resumes with my analytical comments. Please note that formatting cannot be made to match how it would appear on a standard-sized piece of paper. The purpose of providing readers with these examples is to show why strategic decisions were made about content in three sample cases of law school applicants.

Resume #1
Lee Patel, LSAC ID: L44444444

Education:

Master of Science, Syracuse University, 2010

Computer Science with a Concentration in Security[44]

GPA: 3.81

Honors: Certificate of Academic Excellence

Bachelor of Arts *Magna cum Laude,* New York
University,[45] 2006

Major in Philosophy with a Minor in Art

GPA: 3.69; Dean's List (3 Semesters)

Completed freshman year at Jones University: 3.947 GPA;
Provost's List (2 Semesters)

IT Experience:

Contract Security Analyst | Forlorn Security | Atlanta, GA
and Syracuse, NY, May 2009-Present

- Provides recommendations on HIPAA policy and data wiping.
- Forensically investigates data and physical property theft for clients.
- Executes virus scanner software evaluation, installation, and support for multiple platforms.
- Manages accounts for UNIX and Mac OS X.
- Performs wireless network security auditing and penetration testing.

---

[44] This applicant has a few things that are non-traditional. One is that she majored in Philosophy in college but picked something very practical in graduate school, and her experience is largely in IT work.

[45] Lee went to a very good undergraduate school, had a thinking/writing/researching major and did very well.

IT Manager | Big Oil Corporation | Atlanta, GA
March-October 2011
- Supervised daily operations of the IT department.
- Upgraded legacy technology to reduce bottlenecks in business processes.
- Led briefings on new projects, proposals, and budgets.[46]
- Reduced amount of servers, client equipment, and energy needed for daily operations.
- Managed mission critical software upgrade projects.
- Created IT disaster preparedness procedures.[47]
- Created systems audit procedures based on Sarbanes-Oxley.
- Designed new brand website, created a project timeline, and met deployment deadlines.
- Managed development of brand based mobile application projects for iPhone, Android, and Blackberry, from design to rollout.
- Established an online presence for the company brand with Facebook, Twitter, and GasBuddy.

Junior Business Systems Analyst | Starrs Ads | Syracuse, NY June 2007-May 2009
- Administered HP-UX 11.1, Windows 2003, and Mac OS X 10.5 servers.
- Worked closely with finance and accounting departments to troubleshoot technical finance

---

[46] All of the bullet points begin with verbs and there is no reference in the first person.

[47] A lot of IT jobs have overlapping duties, but I did not want the same bullets listed under each job, which is why the list of bullet points for each job gets shorter.

problems (Excel, Access, PeopleSoft, general ledger issues).
- Produced Sarbanes-Oxley audit documentation.
- Collaborated on projects with members of immediate and external departments and managed contracts with outside vendors.
- Led technology presentations for incoming employees and taught help-desk employees advanced technical skills.

Information Technology Coordinator | The Beth Project | New York, NY, 2006–2007[48]
- Acted as Interim Systems Administrator for Windows 2003 server.
- Managed Active Directory by adding, altering, and removing users.
- Trained users on Windows, Mac OS X, and Microsoft Office Suite.
- Presented new software and hardware technologies to staff.
- Drafted and proposed Internet marketing strategy and implemented final versions.
- Designed and created marketing materials using Adobe Create Suite.

---

[48] I would, of course, prefer for there to be months here because it looks like she was at this job from December 2007 to January 2007 written this way. If that were the case, then this is way too long a description for a job that was held for only a month or two.

College Employment:[49]

Independent IT Contractor, New York, NY
Summer - Fall 2007

Associate, Sherwin Williams Paint Store, New York, NY
Summer 2007

Bartender, Tapas Lounge, New York, NY,
Summer 2007

Computer Specialist, Hola Language Center, New York, NY, Summer 2006

Publicity Manager, Syracuse University Summer Studies, Syracuse, NY, Summer 2005

Artistic Endeavors[50]:

Member, NYU Shakespeare Society (acting and directing): *Richard III*, Actor (Buckingham); *Antony and Cleopatra*, Director and Actor (Enobarbus)

Member, Wandering Minds Theater Troupe (acting and promotional materials); *The Duchess of Malfi*, Actor (Delio)

Actor and Director, Willing Suspension Productions; *The Maid's Tragedy*, Actor (Amintor); Edward II, Actor (Mortimer)

Freelance photographer (print and online publications in Syracuse, NY)

Nightcap TV Assistant Producer (Jones University; 2002 – 2003)

---

[49] Lee gets a 2-page resume to account for her significant professional experiences, but bartending and painting jobs don't require the same level of explanations of job duties, especially because they were summer jobs during college. We don't want to mix this in with her professional experience so we have a separate heading.

[50] I would prefer years for these activities, or at least a way to make it more obvious that these activities were during college.

Certifications:

Graduate Certificate in Digital Forensics, Syracuse
    University, May 2010

Graduate Certificate in Information Technology, Syracuse
    University, May 2010

Security Best Practices for Mac OS X 10.4, 2009

Apple Certified Support Professional 10.5, 2008

Apple Certified Technical Coordinator, 2008

Apple Certified Help Desk Specialist, 2007

Interests:[51]

Animal Welfare (Foster cats and contribute to animal
    shelters), 2009-Present

SCUBA and NITROX certified (PADI), 2006-Present

Digital Photography and Editing, 2002-Present

Running, Lifting, Swimming, Yoga, Crossfit, 2002-Present

---

[51] This section shows that Lee is well-rounded. She wanted to write an essay about her dedication to saving feral cats, but I nixed that. It sounded too crazy. Instead, it turned out that Lee had long thought about law school in ways not demonstrated by her resume, and that now was the perfect time for her to go after many years of considering it. She was admitted to several Top 20 schools and is (as of this printing) planning to attend the University of Texas School of Law or Cornell Law School.

Resume #2
Jennifer Simmons, L33333333[52]

Education:

Bachelor of Arts in English
Anticipated May 2013
The University of Iowa
GPA: 3.37
Honors: Dean's List (Spring and Fall 2011)

Experience:

Case Analyst, Chen Law Office, Boise, IA
October 2012–Present
- Works 12–15 hours a week preparing information for lawyers and working with clients to synthesize information for their cases.[53]

Campus Brand Representative, Boise, IA
October 2012–Present
- Works 2-3 hours a week attending events and promoting a new and growing clothing brand targeted at students.[54]

Front Desk Attendant, Holiday Inn, Boise, IA
June 2012–August 2012

---

[52] Jennifer is a pretty traditional college applicant with an OK GPA. She does not have an upward trend in her grades or a higher GPA in her major to highlight.

[53] I would actually prefer Jennifer to add more information here about the type of law the firm does and the level of interaction she has with clients. This job description could definitely be beefed up a bit. One reason it was not is because Jennifer applied to law school in November 2012 so the first two jobs were very new at the time she applied.

[54] For the same reason of timing, this description lacked embellishment. Resume updates should include quantified examples of success in this position such as the increase in sales in the first three months, how her performance compared to other campus reps, etc.

- Worked 20–30 hours a week to help pay for living expenses.

Server, The Italian Restaurant, Boise, IA
    October 2011–May 2012

- Worked 25–35 hours a week in order to help pay for living expenses while attending school full time and studying for the LSAT.[55]

Server, Shintori, Boise, IA
    October 2010–October 2011

- Worked 20– 25 hours a week at a sushi restaurant while attending school full time to help pay for living expenses.

Counselor, Girl Scout Camp, Cimarron, NM
    May 2010–August 2010

- Worked around the clock to greet and train youth and adult participants in limited impact camping, encouraging young women to feel more confident in natural environments.

Activities:

Member, Phi Gamma Beta Sorority
    August 2009–Present

- Serves as head of multicultural committee (January 2012–Present). Planned and coordinated multicultural dinner with four Greek houses and international students.
- Planned and coordinated dance charity event raising $2,600 for the United Way.

---

[55] Because everyone knows what a server does there was no need to explain it. It was more important that we show the number of hours Jennifer was working and that she was handling a lot all at once, and that she did well with the multi-tasking.

- Served as House Maintenance Committee member (October 2010–May 2011).
- Participated in Shack-A-Thon, school-wide charity event benefiting Habitat for Humanity (Fall 2009, 2010, 2011).

Gold Badge Level Girl Scout[56] Achieved in May 2007

- Built a trail for public use in a park outside Cimarron, NM

International Travel:

- Studied abroad in Guadalajara, Mexico,[57] Spring 2009

---

[56] Eagle Scout and the Girl Scout equivalent are sometimes an exception to the "no high school stuff on your resume" rule.

[57] On this, I would like to know more—did she study the language or did she study in English? What is her fluency level in Spanish?

Resume #3
Scott Zhou[58] James L3XXXXXXX

Education:

Bachelor of Arts *summa cum laude,*[59] May 2012

Bobsled University,[60] **College of Liberal Arts and
Sciences** Cumulative GPA: 3.92/4.00

Majors: Philosophy (3.91 GPA); French and Francophone
Studies (4.0 GPA); Minor: English

Honors Concentration in Interdisciplinary Studies

Member of **Phi Beta Kappa** and **Phi Kappa Phi**

Dean's List (all semesters)

Université of Rennes de Bretagne,[61] Summers 2009,
2011

Language and Culture Immersion Program (lived with
host family)

Xiamen University Summer Language Program,
Summer 2010

Language and Culture Program (studied Chinese written
language)

---

[58] This client could choose to be Scott James, but he actually has a multicultural background and this is his middle name. By adding it, it shows another dimension to his background that helps the reader to be curious about him, and this background (growing up living partially in the U.S. and partially in China) is addressed in his diversity statement.

[59] Since Scott went to a school without a prestigious name, we put his degree (Summa honors!) first, then the name of the school on the next line.

[60] I wanted to pick a nondescript, random university without insulting anyone at a particular school, so please forgive the liberty I took in inventing one.

[61] Most people will know this is in France, but it still should've been explicitly stated. Once of the great things about Scott is his fluency in both French and Chinese, and his diversity statement emphasized this in a very cute way, about how he was speaking Chinese in a Chinese restaurant in France, and how it freaked him out when the Chinese lady responded in French. I promise, there was a point to the essay beyond that….but it echoed this part of his resume really nicely.

Employment:

English Teacher, University Immersion Program, China, Spring 2013[62]

*   Teaches English to Chinese college students, lives in local housing and studies advanced written and oral Chinese language program

Varsity Basketball Coach, Georgestone Academy, Jamestown, PA, 2012–2013

*   Organizes practices, develops skills for players individually and as a team, design scouting reports, coaches 30 games per season

Intern, *The Federal News*, Harrisburg, PA, Summer 2008

*   Assisted with the Opinion-Editorial section
*   Wrote an Op-Ed piece on the Tibet-China tension

Activities:

Ambassador, Honors Ambassador, 2012

*   Assisted with all Honors program events for prospective/incoming students

Family Head, Grey Key Society (2 hours/week[63]) 2010–2012

*   Provided tours to prospective students; trained 20 members to give tours
*   Interviewed prospective candidates for membership
*   Received Outstanding Member of October for leadership throughout the interview process

---

[62] Since Scott already graduated from college before applying, he needed to show how he was spending his time in the year after graduation.

[63] Notice how Scott lists the time commitment per week for each activity. Even though some were not especially time consuming, it does go to show he took time to be involved, that he wasn't just about his grades.

Student Advisor, Honors Peer Advisor (1 hour/week),
2010-2012
- Counseled first-year honors students in class choices and helped diversify their schedules

Student Speaker, Orientation Staff, 2010–2011
- Worked with a Freshman Advisor to help first year students adjust to campus life
- Spoke to the group about social and campus life

President, Club Swimming (12 hours/week),
2009–2012
- Communicated with other colleges to organize competitions and team venues
- Arranged practice schedules including developing strength, conditioning, and nutrition plans
- Recruited seven new members
- Posted the fastest 50 and 100 yard freestyle sprints on the team, anchored both 200 freestyle and 400 freestyle relays

Tutor, French/Philosophy (2 hours/week), 2009–2012
- Volunteered as the sole free tutor for the French and Philosophy departments

Project Coordinator, International Service, China,
Summers 2007 and 2008
- Designed program that donated $2,000 to an orphanage sponsoring children with AIDS

Skills:

Multi-Lingual: Speak French (fluent) and Chinese
(conversational)

Pianist, 2001-2008[64]

- Won Pennsylvania state spring festival competition
  on three occasions, received honorable mention at the
  Chopin Competition, and fulfilled requirements to
  teach piano professionally

---

[64] This is another exception to the "no high school on your resume" rule. However, I did not let Scott put his high school basketball achievements or valedictorian status on the resume.

ABOUT THE AUTHOR

Ann K. Levine, Esq. is a law school admission consultant and the founder and chief consultant of Law School Admission Expert, Inc. (www.lawschoolexpert.com) which she established in 2004. In her near-decade as a law school admission consultant, Ann has worked individually with approximately 2,000 applicants, and nearly 100,000 people read her Law School Expert blog each year. The first release of *The Law School Admission Game: Play Like an Expert*, published in 2009, became an Amazon.com bestselling law school guidebook. She is also the author of *The Law School Decision Game: A Playbook for Prospective Lawyers*, in which she surveyed and interviewed more than 250 lawyers to compile advice for people considering attending law school.

After graduating magna cum laude from the University of Miami School of Law in 1999, Ann served as Director of Student Services at the University of Denver College of Law, as Director of Admissions for California Western School of Law, and as Director of Admissions for Loyola Law School in Los Angeles. She has been licensed to practice law in California and Colorado.

Ann lives in Santa Barbara, California, with her husband (an attorney) and their two daughters. When she is not helping people get into law schools across the United States, she is playing tennis. You can follow Ann on Twitter @annlevine and connect with Ann on Facebook at the Law School Admission Expert page for regular updates on law school–related news. Ann personally answers law school admission–related questions on her blog at www.lawschoolexpert.com/blog.

Made in the USA
San Bernardino, CA
06 November 2015